CHINESE VEGETARIAN COOKING

Also by Kenneth H. C. Lo

PEKING COOKING

ILLUSTRATIONS BY TOM FUNK

CHINESE VEGETARIAN COOKING

BY

Kenneth H. C. Lo

PANTHEON BOOKS

A DIVISION OF RANDOM HOUSE, NEW YORK

Library of Congress Cataloging in Publication Data

Lo, Kenneth H. C.
Chinese Vegetarian Cooking.

1. Vegetarianism. 2. Cookery, Chinese. I. Title.
TX837.L55 1974   641.5'636   73-18728
ISBN 0-394-49165-3
ISBN 0-394-70639-0 (pbk.)

Manufactured in the United States of America

987

CONTENTS

NOTE: Recipes for dishes that appear in the text with capital letters (Basic Vegetable Broth, Sweet-and-Sour Sauce, for example) can be found by consulting the Index.

CHINESE
VEGETARIAN
COOKING

INTRODUCTION

COOKING AND SERVING a Chinese meal, whether or not it is vegetarian, presents somewhat different problems from cooking and serving a Western one, since a Chinese meal is usually communal. It is rather like a hot buffet with a great variety of dishes, or a banquet, involving a dozen or more courses. The major task is therefore to produce several dishes to serve at the same time, for a family meal, or a series of dishes served one after another, for a party meal or banquet. Unlike the task of producing soup or first course, main course, and dessert for a Western meal, a Chinese meal involves a much greater number of dishes: four to six for a family meal, and a dozen or more for a banquet. The element of display, which is an important component, makes Chinese vegetable cooking almost a flower show in its visual appeal. A great profusion of colors is possible partly because with the Chinese method vegetables are never overcooked, which kills their freshness and color, but are treated like a series of "hot salads." Vegetables can be presented singly, with an eye to purity, or assembled together, often after a minimal amount of cooking, or prepared by several different methods in order to achieve the most attractive orchestration of color, texture, and flavor.

Since a Chinese meal consists of several substantial dishes and/or several courses, it is difficult to specify the number of servings any single dish will provide. Generally, for the recipes here, I have assumed that the dish will be accompanied by two to three others, which will be shared by four to six people.

The diversity of texture in Chinese cooking often derives from the different methods of cooking different ingredients: deep-fried foods are crisp, stewed or simmered foods are tender and saucy, while quick-fried foods are fresh and crunchy. Variety and balance come from the careful blending of flavors resulting from the choice of materials and the superimposition of one type of flavor upon another, such as dried or salted foods on fresh foods, or meat on vegetables; or through the common practice of impregnating hot oil with the flavor of strong vegetables (ginger, garlic, onion), and then using it to cook and flavor the main component of the dish. The flavoring agents — such as wine, bean paste, bean-curd cheese, soy sauce, hoisin sauce, meat broths, and sugar — are usually introduced only during the concluding stages of the cooking.

When we embarked on this book, it occurred to both my publisher and myself that it would be best to divide and group the material under the different methods of cooking, and then to subdivide it further into the different vegetables employed, or into the different main groups of dishes being produced (soups, salads, desserts, starches, etc.).

In spite of the widespread popularity of Chinese food, Chinese cooking is still rather new and strange to the average Western housewife. By concentrating each chapter on one method of cooking, the book should make it much easier for the Westerner to conduct an initial "trial," after which the mystique still surrounding Chinese cooking should evaporate. One of the purposes of this book, apart from introducing Chinese vegetable and vegetarian cooking, is to help dispel some of the mystery that still pervades any subject connected with the Chinese.

For handy reference, a selected list of the major vegetables included in this book, with some of the recipes in which they can be used, has been provided in the Quick Guide on pages 14–17.

With Chinese cooking, as with any other, the principal factors involved are cutting, flavoring, and heating. Once these are mastered, all that is needed is experience and increasing acquaintance in cooking and eating. Because of the Chinese practice of marrying one type of food to another, and super-imposing one type of flavoring or method of cooking on an-other, the number of dishes that can be concocted is a ques-tion of permutation, which means that the repertoire at the cook's command is almost limitless. A whole new culinary world is open to the cook who learns the fundamentals of cutting, flavoring, and heating that have afforded countless millions and generations of Chinese unfailing pleasure.

One other point should be elaborated before I conclude this Introduction: although in Chinese cooking, as in West-ern cooking, there is a definite distinction between a vegetari-an and a nonvegetarian dish, the distinction between a meat dish and a vegetable dish is only a matter of degree. Thus, in Chinese cuisine, a vegetable dish is one in which a vegetable constitutes more than three-quarters of the weight of all the ingredients; a meat dish is one in which meat provides more than a quarter of the weight. Both vegetable and meat are present in some combination in the majority of Chinese dish-es, and in a book like this, which is about Chinese cooking as well as vegetarian cooking, such dishes should be represent-ed. Therefore, for every applicable series of vegetarian dishes, I have indicated nonvegetarian parallels. Since in most cases the methods of cooking employed are almost exactly the same—the difference being only a matter of flavoring or the addition of some shredded or thinly sliced meat at some point in the process—the suggestions for incorporating a few key ingredients should make each situation or process amply clear. However, because this book is centered on vegetables, all the nonvegetarian dishes included are still predominantly vegetable in character.

Since this book is designed for use in the average Western kitchen—vegetarian or otherwise—its aims are purely practi-cal. Consequently, it offers no apology for making fairly free use of such foods as dairy products (milk, cream, cheese, etc.), which are not often employed in Chinese cookery, except in frontier regions, but which certainly can sometimes be used to advantage. There are other concessions to the modern kitchen, where modern equipment such as the electric blender, pressure cooker, thermostatically controlled oven, and even the can opener can help to simplify difficult or laborious operations.

Times change, and so can Chinese cooking.

Those who master Chinese vegetable cooking will find that the profusion of tastes, shapes, colors, and textures creates a veritable garden on the dining table. Such an attractive array might well tempt some to greater efforts in the garden outdoors. With the prospect of such a delicious reward for their efforts, many people may dig with greater heart to produce the vegetable dishes that they will enjoy and that will be acclaimed by all who share them.

CUTTING, HEATING,
AND FLAVORING

Cutting, heating, and flavoring are the three basic processes in preparing food. Initially, it may seem that they could hardly vary much from one cuisine to another. After all, there are only so many ways of cutting, heating, or flavoring food. But when one observes and considers each of the processes in detail, the possibility of finesse is considerable, and when one form of finesse is combined with another, the variety of end products that can result is impressive. It is the exploitation of the subtleties within each of these basic processes and their combination that makes Chinese cooking so wide-ranging and distinctive. Yet we must not allow this "wheels within wheels" concept of Chinese cooking to develop into a mystique that may obscure the fact that it is basically quite simple, and that Chinese vegetable and vegetarian cooking is even simpler, for it is only a part of the larger whole. Incongruous though it may sound, Chinese cooking is like riding a bicycle. Once you can mount a bicycle and stay on it, you can do almost anything with it, even if you do not fully understand the complex relation of forces between one wheel and another. So too with Chinese cooking.

Since in neither cooking nor bicycling are we trying to probe the truth of the universe, we must quickly come down to essentials, and the "brass tacks" of Chinese cooking techniques are:

CUTTING

In Chinese cooking, cutting takes two things into consideration: the type of heat being used and the shape of the principal substance to be cooked. If the latter is long or elongated (noodles, for instance) the supplementary materials are cut in more or less the same elongated shape. If the principal substance is square or round (such as peas), the other materials are also chopped or diced into small pieces of more or less the same size. If the food is to be cooked for a considerable time (two or three hours), all the cutting necessary is a little trimming, and if the supplementary materials are added at the outset, they too require only a minimum of cutting or trimming. If, however, they are added toward the end of the cooking, or if the main substance is already cooked, then they will have to be reduced to a much smaller size — or even minced — before they are added. (Chopped or minced chives or spring onions are sprinkled over many Chinese dishes before serving.)

A large number of Chinese dishes are cooked by stir frying, a method that takes only seconds or at most a minute or two. Foods cooked in this way must be able to heat through rapidly. To facilitate this, they are usually shredded, cut into very thin slices, or chopped into cubes the size of a lump of sugar or smaller. Leaf vegetables are cut into 1 – 2-inch pieces; firm vegetables are often "rolling cut" — sliced diagonally or slantwise after each quarter turn so that a larger surface can be exposed to heating and flavoring. Large chunks of foods that have been cooked for a fairly long time are often cut into bite-size pieces before serving, which makes them easier to handle with chopsticks.

HEATING

Except for stir frying, which is uniquely Chinese, the methods used in Chinese cooking are basically much the same as those used in Western cooking: boiling, stewing, deep frying, shallow frying, roasting, baking, steaming, grilling, barbecuing, smoking, etc. In addition, there are a few specialized forms of heat treatment, such as hot burying (in salt, mud, or sand), hot splashing (with oil), dry scorching (on a dry metal plate or griddle), and simmering in herbal broth (hot marinading). Some recipes require "drunken marinading," which is not a heat treatment, but a cold flavoring technique used to complete a cooking process. But it is in the subdivisions under each category, and in the use of one method in conjunction with another, that Chinese cooking begins to exploit its potential. The methods commonly used are briefly explained below; they are described in greater detail in the appropriate places later in the book.

BOILING

Plunged boiling: thinly sliced material is plunged into boiling water or broth for a very short period of time and then taken out for immediate eating.

Deep boiling: food is boiled in quantities of water with no seasoning and dipped in piquant sauces when eaten.

Long simmering: food is simmered over very low heat with or without many flavoring materials.

Foods prepared in these ways without flavoring materials are usually further cooked by quick deep fry and then eaten with sauce, or sliced and further cooked for a short period in a small casserole together with selected flavoring materials.

STEWING

Red cooking: food is cooked with soy sauce.

White cooking: food is cooked in light-colored broth (occasionally with milk, cream, or beaten egg white added).

Hot assembly: this is actually a short form of stewing, in which a number of foods and ingredients are cooked separately by different methods and then assembled in a pot or casserole and cooked together for a short period of time along with a few selected flavoring ingredients.

STEAMING

Open steaming: foods (often seasoned and marinaded) are steamed in an open dish for a comparatively short but intense period (five to twenty-five minutes).

Closed steaming: foods are steamed in a covered heatproof dish for long periods (an hour or two or more). This process, which is not unlike double-boiler cooking, ensures an even temperature throughout the whole cooking period.

Terminal steaming: steaming here serves as a sealing process by which foods already cooked by other methods (such as stir frying, or braising) are assembled for further tenderizing by high-intensity steaming.

DEEP FRYING

Plain deep frying

Battered deep frying

Short-period deep frying: this preliminary or initial process is followed by another method of cooking (such as stir frying, braising, hot assembling). Short deep frying is to plain deep frying as parboiling is to boiling.

Deep frying as a concluding process: this is employed after a period of steaming, long simmering, or marinading.

SHALLOW FRYING

A Western process typical of shallow frying is frying bread. In Chinese cooking, it is the usual method of crisping up one part of the food (usually the bottom), which has already been cooked in another way—by stir frying or steaming (as in the case of Cantonese fried noodles, or Peking pot-stuck "raviolis"). In addition to crisping, shallow frying also ensures that the dish is cooked through. If you are short of oil, shallow frying can do the work of deep frying if you simply turn the food around in the hot oil in the pan.

ROASTING AND BAKING

Roasting and baking are seldom used for vegetable cooking in China, partly because few Chinese kitchens are equipped with an oven, and where there is one, it is usually reserved for cooking poultry or meat. But the average Western kitchen has an oven, which can easily be adapted for Chinese cooking by using a casserole for:

POT ROASTING

SLOW OPEN ROASTING (FOR SUCH FOODS AS SWEET POTATOES)

HOT ASSEMBLY (IN A CASSEROLE)

BAKING (WRAPPED IN ALUMINUM FOIL)

BAKING (AS A DRYING AND CRISPING PROCESS—AFTER BRAISING OR STEWING)

GRILLING AND BARBECUING

Grilling and barbecuing are also processes chiefly associated with meat cooking. In vegetable cooking, they can usually be used in place of scorch frying, where a slightly burned taste is required, or of dry frying, where a drying-up, reducing process can be speeded up before the final stir fry.

SMOKING

Smoking is seldom used in cooking vegetables. Usually when a smoky flavor is desired in a vegetable dish, it is achieved by introducing a material such as smoked meat during cooking.

STIR FRYING

Stir frying is probably the most widely used method of cooking in China. It can be divided into several subcategories or combined with a few other processes:

QUICK STIR FRYING (plain)   STIR FRYING AND STEAMING

DRY STIR FRYING *(kan shao)*   STIR FRYING AND HOT ASSEMBLY

WET STIR FRYING *(liao)*   STIR FRYING AND SCORCH FRYING

STIR FRYING AND BRAISING

HOT AND COLD TOSSING

Tossing (or *pan*) is the process of tossing food, as in salad making. In this case, raw or parboiled vegetables or cooked noodles are tossed in cold or, more frequently, hot dressings and sauces.

HOT MARINADING (OR SIMMERING) IN HERBAL MASTER SAUCE (LU)

It is a common practice in Chinese cooking to prepare a strong herbal broth with a soy-sauce base in which foods are immersed and simmered for varying periods of time, until cooked. This is often followed by a further short period of cooking (by stir frying, deep frying, or steaming). The subtlety of the flavor is varied by slightly varying the contents of the herbal Master Sauce and by using other flavors in the final cooking.

FLAVORING

In Chinese food preparation, flavorings are used in three stages:

before cooking, as marinades

during cooking, through sauces and seasonings

after cooking, through condiments in the form of dips and mixes on the table.

Some of the principal categories of flavorers are:

Basic seasonings: salt, pepper, sugar, vinegar, chili, curry, five-spice powder, mustard, sesame oil (aromatic)

Strong vegetables: onions, scallions (spring onions), ginger, garlic

Soybean products: soy sauce, black beans (salted), soybean paste (yellow and black), bean-curd cheese (red and yellow)

Other sauces: hoisin, plum, chili, tomato, and two nonvegetarian sauces — shrimp and oyster

Dried, pickled, and salted vegetables: dried mushrooms, salted cabbage, red-in-snow (pickled cabbage), Szechuan cabbage (hot), dried bamboo shoots, dried lily-bud stems (golden needles), wood ears, dried lotus root, dried tangerine peel, preserved turnip

Miscellaneous: sesame paste (peanut butter can be used as a substitute), various wines.

In Chinese vegetable and vegetarian cooking, quite a number of Western products are both convenient and useful: yeast extract (Marmite), and all the various pickles, chutneys, jams, and preserves. For nonvegetarians a chicken-stock cube can be conveniently used in the preparation of many dishes, for in Chinese cooking one of the most widely used nonvegetarian flavorers is concentrated chicken or meat broth or meat gravy (from meat cooked with soy sauce).

With the proper pan on the burner (gas is preferable to electricity), and all the usual seasonings in the kitchen cupboard — salt, pepper, vinegar, sugar, mustard, tomato purée — plus soy sauce, chili sauce, and Vegetable Broth, you should be ready to begin cooking Chinese vegetable or vegetarian dishes. If possible, you should also try to have on hand Chinese salted black beans, bean-curd cheese, hoisin sauce, sesame paste (or peanut butter), sesame oil, and Chinese dried mushrooms (one of the most frequently used items in Chinese vegetable and vegetarian cooking).

For nonvegetarians, added supplies are: concentrated chicken broth, made by adding a chicken-stock cube to chicken broth, shrimp sauce, oyster sauce, fish sauce, and some red-cooked meat (cooked in soy sauce) with gravy.

This book is dedicated to all lovers of vegetables (including all vegetarians who enjoy their diet), but *not* to those who have taken to vegetables because they abhor meat and have to put up with vegetables by default. It is dedicated to all those who think that vegetables are one of God's gifts to man and as such should be thoroughly enjoyed and appreciated.

QUICK GUIDE

ALTHOUGH EATING CHINESE has become familiar to Western-ers living in even quite small towns, cooking Chinese may still be thought of as something rather exotic. To enable the cook to start with the known, here is a selected list of recipes whose main ingredient is one of the more commonly available vegetables.

ASPARAGUS Stir-Braised Asparagus (p. 31); Deep-fried Mari-naded Asparagus (p. 42); Hot-Marinaded Deep-Fried Eggplant or Asparagus Tips (p. 58); Clear-Simmered Asparagus (p. 79); Asparagus and Bamboo-Shoot Soup (p. 98)

BEAN SPROUTS Plain Stir-Fried Bean Sprouts (p. 22)

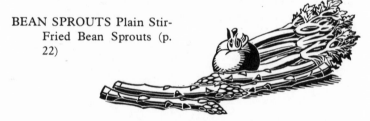

BROCCOLI Stir-Braised Broccoli (p. 29); Deep-Fried Marinaded Broccoli (p. 42); Steamed Broccoli with Fu-Yung Sauce (p. 45); Red-Cooked Broccoli (p. 65); White-Cooked Broccoli (p. 70); Clear-Simmered Broccoli (p. 77); Broccoli Soup (p. 99)

BRUSSELS SPROUTS Stir-Braised Brussels Sprouts (p. 30); Deep-Fried Mari-naded Brussels Sprouts (p. 42); Red-Cooked Brussels Sprouts (p. 65); White-Cooked Brussels Sprouts (p. 70); Clear-Simmered Brussels Sprouts (p. 78); Brussels Sprout Soup (p. 98)

CABBAGE Stir-Braised Cabbage (p. 30); Quick Deep-Fried and Stir-Fried Chinese or Savoy Cabbage (p. 37); Quick Deep-Fried Sweet-and-Sour Chinese or Savoy Cabbage (p. 38); Steamed Cabbage with Stems (p. 46); Hot-Marinaded Cabbage with Sweet-and-Sour Sauce (p. 61); Red-Cooked Cabbage (p. 66); White-Cooked Cabbage (p. 69); Clear-Simmered Chinese or Green Cabbage (p. 77); Hot Cabbage Soup (p. 96); Heart of Cabbage Soup (p. 97); Cabbage and Celery Mustard Salad (p. 150)

CARROTS Stir-Braised Carrots (p. 31); Steamed Parsnips and Carrots in Hot Peanut-Butter Sauce (p. 51); Hot-Marinaded Carrots and Turnips (p. 56); Hot-Marinaded Shredded Carrots (p. 62); Red-Cooked Carrots and/or Turnips (p. 67); Carrot, Watercress, and Cucumber Vegetable Rice (p. 109); Chinese Carrot Salad (p. 149)

CAULIFLOWER Stir-Braised Cauliflower (p. 29); Quick Deep-Fried Cauliflower (in Batter) (p. 36); Deep-Fried Marinaded Cauliflower (p. 42); White-Cooked Cauliflower (p. 70); Cauliflower Fu-Yung (p. 131).

CELERY Plain Stir-Fried Celery (p. 23); Quick Deep-Fried Celery (p. 38); Hot-Marinaded Celery Stir Fried with Chinese Dried Mushrooms (p. 57); Red-Cooked Celery (p. 66); White-Cooked Celery (p. 70); Clear-Simmered Celery (p. 77); Celery Soup (p. 94); Cabbage and Celery Mustard Salad (p. 150)

CUCUMBER Strips of Cucumber Soup (p. 90)

EGGPLANT Stir-Braised Eggplant (p. 31); Quick Deep-Fried Eggplant (p. 36); Deep-Fried Marinaded Eggplant (p. 42); Hot-Marinaded Deep-Fried Eggplant (p. 58); Red-Cooked Eggplant (p. 64)

GREEN BEANS Plain Stir-Fried Young Beans or Snow Peas (p. 26); Stir-Braised Green Beans (p. 30); Quick Deep-Fried and Stir-Fried Green Beans (p. 39); Steamed Green Beans in Hot Peanut-Butter Sauce (p. 52); Hot-Marinaded Stir-Fried Green Beans (p. 56); White-Cooked Green Beans (p. 70); Green Beans Fu-Yung (p. 131); Bean Curd Stir Fried with Green Beans (p. 140); Clear-Simmered Green Beans (p. 78)

LEEKS Plain Stir-Fried Young Leeks (p. 23); Leek Soup (p. 94)

LETTUCE Plain Stir-Fried Lettuce (p. 23); Quick-Steamed Buttered Lettuce (p. 44); Lettuce Soup (p. 95); Clear-Simmered Bean Curd with Lettuce (p. 146)

MUSHROOMS Quick Deep-Fried and Quick-Fried Button Mushrooms (p. 41); Deep-Fried Marinaded Mushrooms (p. 41); Mushroom Sauce (p. 85); Mushroom Soup (p. 93); Green-Pea and Mushroom Vegetable Rice (p. 108)

ONION Chinese Onion Soup (p. 100)

PARSNIPS Steamed Parsnips and Carrots in Hot Peanut-Butter Sauce (p. 51)

PEAS Plain Stir-Fried Green Peas (p. 28); Sweet Pea Soup (p. 102); Green-Pea Soup (p. 104); Green-Pea and Mushroom Vegetable Rice (p. 108)

POTATOES Glazed Potato Chips (p. 170)

SPINACH Plain Stir-Fried Spinach (p. 21); Stir-Fried Eggs with Spinach (p. 129); Bean Curd Stir Fried with Spinach (p. 139); Spinach Soup (p. 91); Green Jade Soup (p. 92)

TOMATOES Plain Stir-Fried Tomatoes (p. 25); Tomato Soup (p. 93)

TURNIPS Hot-Marinaded Carrots and Turnips (p. 56); Red-Cooked Turnips (p. 67); Turnip Soup (p. 97)

WATERCRESS Watercress Soup (p. 94)

ZUCCHINI Stir-Braised Zucchini (p. 31); Quick Deep-Fried Zucchini (p. 36); White Cooked Zucchini (p. 70); Steamed Zucchini Bowl (p. 48); Clear-Simmered Zucchini (p. 78)

NOTE ON VEGETABLE BROTH

Many of the recipes in this book call for Vegetable Broth. Ideally, this should be the Basic Vegetable Broth (page 89). However, as this takes some time to prepare, suitable alternatives are the Simplified Vegetable Broth (see page 90) or one of these two substitutes:

Dissolve 1 vegetable-stock cube and 1 teaspoon vegetable concentrate (Instant Vege Base or the equivalent) in 3 cups hot water

Add 1 tablespoon soy sauce, 1 teaspoon yeast extract (Marmite), and 1½ teaspoons vegetable concentrate to 3 cups hot water; stir until completely dissolved

These products can be obtained from health-food shops.

STIR FRYING AND DEEP FRYING

STIR FRYING consists of cooking foods that have been cut into thin slices (or into shreds) in a small quantity of oil (usually 2–4 tablespoons) in a frying pan over high heat. Because of the high heat, the food cooks rapidly and must be turned, scrambled, and stirred continuously to prevent sticking and scorching. This method of cooking is also called quick frying. A more graphic and complete description of the process would be "quick stir frying."

The process usually starts with heating the oil—a vegetable oil such as peanut or corn—in the middle of the pan and adding a small quantity of a few strongly flavored vegetables, such as onion, garlic, and ginger (or any one of them). These are fried and stirred in the oil for a minute or less. This first stage impregnates the oil with the palate-stimulating flavor of these strong vegetables.

In the second stage, the main ingredient, which has been

shredded or sliced thin, is added to the flavor-impregnated oil. It is then turned in the hot oil for 1 – 2 minutes (the length of time depends on the quantity; if the amount is more than 1 pound, an extra 1 – 2 minutes may be required). If salt is sprinkled over the vegetables at this stage, and they are stirred vigorously, they will often turn greener.

It is usually in the third stage that the flavorers are added: for vegetarians, Vegetable Broth, soy sauce, soybean paste, sugar, wine, hoisin sauce, tomato sauce, chili sauce, vinegar, mustard, bean-curd cheese, or sesame oil (for aroma); for nonvegetarians, concentrated chicken broth, meat gravy, shrimp sauce, etc. Adding these ingredients at this stage imparts more flavor to the food and also helps to prevent it from scorching.

For foods and vegetables that do not require prolonged cooking, this is the final stage of the cooking. After a few more rapid turns and stirrings, the food can be put into a well-heated serving dish and served. The water has been released from the vegetable by its contact with the hot oil and hot metal of the pan and combines with the flavorers to produce ample sauce. The swift cooking makes for freshness, and the ingredients retain much of their original food value.

Where more than one main ingredient is combined in the cooking, it is usual to add the one that requires longer cooking to the impregnated oil for 1 – 2 minutes of stir frying, then to push it to the sides of the pan and add a little more oil before putting the other ingredients in the middle of the pan. The second group of ingredients is stir fried for a few minutes, then mixed with the first, and combined with the flavorers in the general final stirring. Quite often, even when a single vegetable is being cooked, the firmer parts, such as the stalk, stem, or root (thinly sliced), are put into the pan and cooked for an initial period before the tender leaves are added. If high heat is used, as is often the case, some broth may have to be added to the first ingredients to prevent scorching.

With hard vegetables, such as asparagus, broccoli, carrots, turnips, green beans, and potatoes, parboiling may be advisable before stir frying. In the case of the semihard vegetables, such as cabbage, celery, bamboo shoots, cauliflower, eggplant, zucchini, and brussels sprouts, a short final period of braising is all that is required to tenderize them.

After the vegetables have been stir fried, a little more liquid is added, and the pan is covered. The braising should be carefully timed, and may last 2–5 minutes, but the cover should be removed only once before the final stirring and serving. (Lifting the cover frequently tends to make vegetables turn yellow.)

Simple quick stir frying without parboiling or braising is ideal for soft vegetables or vegetables that require very little cooking. These include spinach, lettuce, bean sprouts, young leeks, watercress, young hearts of savoy cabbage, tomatoes, sliced cucumbers, garden peas, and snow peas.

For the various kinds of stir frying, the best pan is one that is large and deep sided and has a close-fitting lid (both for short braising and to prevent splashing). It should not be heavy, for in Chinese stir-fry cooking, the heat should be conducted by the pan as swiftly as possible. A thick iron pan is also too heavy to be handled with dexterity.

Deep frying is the second major kind of frying used in Chinese cooking. While it is commonly considered to be limited to foods that have been dipped in a batter, or to foods wrapped in a dough skin—which we will deal with later in this book—it is also extremely successful in cooking vegetables without batter. The speed of the process appeals naturally to the Chinese palate, which finds crisp, crunchy textures appetizing, on their own or in combination with softer textures.

As for stir frying, a vegetable oil—preferably peanut oil—is used for deep frying. More oil is required than in stir frying; depending on the size of the pot used, as much as 1–2 cups may be needed. However, the thrifty need not worry; it can often be reused. The fat should reach a depth of about 2 inches, in order to permit the food to float to the top when it is done.

In the recipes that follow, deep frying will be used as an independent method, and also in combination with other processes. This is part of the Chinese tradition of blending to achieve the best.

PLAIN OR QUICK STIR-FRIED DISHES

These dishes are cooked for only a brief period. Natural-ly, the vegetables suitable for this kind of cooking are those that are natively tender. Plain stir-fried vegetables retain their original freshness, while offering subtle enhancements in flavor.

PLAIN STIR-FRIED SPINACH

1¼ lb spinach
1 small onion
2 cloves garlic
2 slices ginger root
3 – 4 Tb vegetable oil
½ tsp salt
1 Tb sherry
1½ Tb soy sauce
1 tsp sugar
½ Tb sesame oil (optional)

Preparation
Remove the hard stems of the spinach, and then cut or tear the leaves into 1½ – 2-inch squares. Mince the onion. Crush garlic and shred ginger.

Cooking
Heat the vegetable oil in a large frying pan. Add onion, gar-lic, and ginger. Stir fry for 1 minute over high heat. Add the spinach and sprinkle with salt. Spread the spinach over the pan. Turn and stir the spinach in the oil for about 2 – 3 min-utes, until it is well coated. Add sherry, soy sauce, and sugar. Continue to turn and stir more gently over medium heat for another 2 – 3 minutes. Add sesame oil, and turn the vegetable over once more. Place on a very well-heated serving dish. Serves 4 – 6.

For nonvegetarians, the only difference will be to use ½ crushed chicken-stock cube during the second stage of the stir frying and 1 tablespoon melted lard or chicken fat at the final stage.

Alternative Combinations

Stir-fried spinach can be combined with many other vegetables, but most often with mushrooms. Before the spinach is cooked, ¼ pound fresh mushrooms may be added. Slice the caps in half and stir fry for 2 minutes in 1½ extra tablespoons oil or butter. Push them to the sides of the pan before the spinach is added. Dried mushrooms should be soaked in hot water for ½ hour and the stems discarded.

For nonvegetarians, ¼ pound thinly sliced meat (beef, lamb, pork) may be used instead of mushrooms, especially when the meal contains no big meat dish. Connoisseurs, however, prefer the plain fried spinach.

PLAIN STIR-FRIED BEAN SPROUTS

Bean sprouts can be stir fried in precisely the same manner as the spinach in the previous recipe. For 1¼ pounds bean sprouts, use the same quantities of the other ingredients; the cooking time is the same, although bean sprouts may be cooked for a slightly shorter period. Before serving, 1 tablespoon chopped chives or spring onions may be sprinkled over the dish.

Alternative Combinations

Bean sprouts are most often combined with Chinese dried mushrooms or dried bamboo shoots, which must be soaked in hot water for ½ hour and shredded. For 1 pound bean sprouts, use about ⅙–¼ pound dried bamboo shoots and an extra tablespoon oil. If meat is combined with the bean sprouts, it too must be cut into thin shreds. Stir fry for 2–3 minutes in an extra tablespoon oil and ½ teaspoon salt before adding the bean sprouts to the pan. Adding 1 – 2 teaspoons shrimp sauce or fish sauce greatly enhances the flavor.

Another vegetable that is often combined with bean sprouts is chili pepper. After the seeds have been removed, the pepper is usually shredded and added to the oil with the garlic, onions, etc., for a short period of stir frying before the bean sprouts are introduced. The result – Hot Plain Stir-Fried Bean Sprouts – is a piquant dish.

PLAIN STIR-FRIED LETTUCE

Lettuce can be treated in precisely the same manner as spinach, but it requires even less cooking (1½ – 2 minutes will be sufficient). Lettuce prepared in this way can also be combined with fresh mushrooms or Chinese dried mushrooms that have been soaked for ½ hour in hot water.

PLAIN STIR-FRIED YOUNG LEEKS

When the Chinese cook leeks, they use the entire green part. To prepare young leeks for plain stir frying, cut diagonally into approximately 2-inch lengths. Add the green parts to the stir fry about 1 minute after the white parts. Since they are strong tasting, leeks benefit from 1 – 2 tablespoons Vegetable Broth added at the second stage.

For nonvegetarians, leeks are usually combined with strong-flavored meats, such as beef or lamb, which should be cut into the same length as the leeks and sliced very thinly; these are put into the stir fry a minute before the leeks.

PLAIN STIR-FRIED CELERY

Although celery is a somewhat harder vegetable than young leeks, it requires no more cooking. Treat it in the same way as any of the other above vegetables: slice it diagonally into 1½-inch segments. When celery is cooked along with other vegetables, it is usually combined with 1-2 shredded chili peppers to produce a hot dish. The peppers are added to the stir fry along with onion, ginger, and garlic before the celery is put into the pan. During the second stage of the cooking, 1-2 tablespoons butter make a welcome addition.

For nonvegetarians, celery can be stir fried with sliced pork, beef, lamb, bacon, or ham. The meat should be stir fried for 1-2 minutes (2½-3 minutes for pork) before the celery is added.

WATERCRESS AND ENDIVE

These two vegetables are used in the West mainly for salads. However, they can be stir fried in the same manner as celery or young leeks (see above). During the early stage of the stir frying, 1 tablespoon hoisin sauce, 1 tablespoon peanut butter, and tomato purée can be added. Watercress is seldom prepared and eaten on its own. Usually it is chopped and used as a garnish (in the same manner as spring onions and chives) for other vegetables and for meat dishes. A typical use for watercress is as a garnish for a dish of stir-fried tomatoes.

PLAIN STIR-FRIED TOMATOES

8 firm medium-size tomatoes
4-inch piece cucumber
2 stalks spring onions
2 cloves garlic
2 slices ginger root
3 Tb vegetable oil
½ tsp salt
2 Tb butter
3 Tb soy sauce
½ Tb soybean paste
2 tsp sugar
1 Tb hoisin sauce
2 Tb dry sherry
2 Tb chopped watercress

Preparation
Plunge the tomatoes briefly in boiling water, then skin them. Slice each tomato vertically into quarters. Slice the cucumber into 2-inch lengths and then lengthwise into thin slices; do not remove the skin. Chop the spring onions, including the green parts, into ¼-inch segments. Crush the garlic and ginger.

Cooking
Heat the oil in a frying pan. When hot, add the garlic, ginger, and spring onions. Stir fry for ½ minute. Add the salt, butter, and cucumber. Stir fry for 1½ minutes. Add the tomatoes, soy sauce, soybean paste, sugar, and hoisin sauce. Turn gently in the oil and sauce for 2 minutes. Pour in the sherry. Turn and stir gently for another 1½ minutes. Sprinkle with chopped watercress.

PLAIN STIR-FRIED CHINESE CABBAGE

In texture, Chinese cabbage lies somewhere between lettuce and celery, but it has a distinctive tang. It can be treated just like celery, which means that it does not need much cooking, and it is tasty enough to stand on its own and be cooked in the same way as Plain Stir-Fried Spinach. Chinese cabbage is often cooked "hot" — with 1–2 shredded chili peppers added to the oil during the early stage of the stir frying. As an alternative, shredded Chinese dried mushrooms (soaked for ½ hour in hot water) can be added, along with 1–2 tablespoons butter, and 1 tablespoon hoisin sauce, all put in at the second stage of the stir frying.

For nonvegetarians, Chinese cabbage is often stir fried together with thinly sliced meat (¼–½ pound pork, chicken, beef, or lamb), which is added to the pan 1–2 minutes before the cabbage. The meat may require some slight seasoning (½ teaspoon salt or 1 tablespoon soy sauce, and pepper to taste) before it is put into the pan. When it has cooked for 1–2 minutes, push the meat to the sides of the pan so that the main vegetable can be stir fried in the middle. When it is ready, the meat, which has been cooking longer, is scooped or stirred back into the middle to combine with the vegetable. For the final stirring 1–2 tablespoons Vegetable Broth, soy sauce, and sherry may be added. It is at this last stage that adjustments in seasonings can be made if necessary. A minute quantity of aromatic or enriching oil, such as sesame oil or chicken fat, may be added to give interest and distinction to the dish.

Ordinary cabbage, such as savoy, can be cooked in a similar way, but it will require an extra 3–4 minutes of sautéing over low to medium heat before a final tossing and stirring up.

PLAIN STIR-FRIED YOUNG BEANS OR SNOW PEAS

So long as they are young and tender, green beans and snow peas can be stir fried with great success. Unlike spinach, leeks, and celery, which are not overpowered by the strongly flavored garlic, ginger, and onion, the more delicate green beans and snow peas are best cooked largely on their own.

1 lb green beans or snow peas
2 Tb vegetable oil
½ tsp salt
4 Tb Vegetable Broth
2 Tb butter
1 Tb soy sauce
½ Tb hoisin sauce
1 tsp sugar blended with 1 tsp cornstarch
    in 2 Tb water
1½ Tb sherry

Preparation

Wash, dry, trim off ends, and remove strings from the beans or snow peas, if necessary.

Cooking

Heat the oil in a frying pan. Add salt. Stir a few times Add the beans or snow peas. Stir fry gently over moderate heat for 2 minutes. Add Vegetable Broth, butter, soy sauce, and hoisin sauce, and continue to stir fry gently for 3 minutes. Add sugar blended with cornstarch and water, and sherry. Stir and turn the vegetables for another minute and serve. Because the stir frying here is gentle, the process is akin to, and can be described as, sautéing.

Alternative Combinations

This is such a pure dish of glistening green that the only extraneous element one can introduce without destroying its purity is the dark-brown richness of Chinese dried black mushrooms. These must be soaked in hot water for ½ hour and their stems removed. Then add 6–8 pieces, along with the beans and 1 additional tablespoon oil, and an additional ½ tablespoon butter. Stir and cook gently together with the beans for 6–8 minutes.

This dish is not suited to the addition of any meat, but concentrated chicken broth may be substituted for Vegetable Broth. On the other hand, green beans or snow peas prepared in this way can be used to garnish dishes that are mainly meat.

PLAIN STIR-FRIED GREEN PEAS

1 lb fresh or frozen green peas
1 Tb dried bean curd (optional)
4 Chinese dried black mushrooms
2 oz bamboo shoots
3 Tb butter
1/2 tsp salt
2 Tb vegetable oil
4 Tb Vegetable Broth
1/2 tsp white bean-curd cheese
1 Tb soy sauce
2 tsp sugar
1 Tb sherry

Preparation
Thaw the peas if frozen. Soak the dried bean curd in hot water for 1 hour. Soak the Chinese mushrooms in hot water for 1/2 hour. Remove and discard the stalks and dice the mushrooms into approximately the same size as the peas. Dice the bamboo shoots and dried bean curd into pieces of approximately the same size.

Cooking
Heat the butter in a frying pan. When hot, add the salt and the peas. Stir fry over medium heat for 2 minutes. Meanwhile heat the oil in a smaller pan over a high flame. Add the diced mushrooms, bamboo shoots, and dried bean curd, and stir fry over high heat for 2 minutes. Pour the contents of the smaller pan into the larger pan containing the peas. Add the Vegetable Broth, bean-curd cheese, soy sauce, sugar, and sherry. Stir fry gently on low heat for 4 – 5 minutes more. Adjust for seasoning.

STIR FRYING AND BRAISING OR SAUTÉING

This is simply an extension of the process of quick stir frying in which harder vegetables are given an extra period

(3 – 5 minutes) of braising under cover. Generally, this means that an additional quantity of liquid (Vegetable Broth if vegetarian; chicken stock if not) is added, and a tight-fitting cover is put on the frying pan for a further period of cooking over low or medium heat. The heat may be raised again for the final stirring, when the cover is removed, and small quantities of wine and aromatic oil are added (or for nonvegetarians chicken fat or lard). It is usually the semihard vegetables, such as broccoli, green beans, brussels sprouts, savoy cabbage, cauliflower, chicory, peppers, eggplant, and zucchini, that are cooked in this way. Apart from its tenderizing effect, the extra cooking time also allows the flavors of the different ingredients to mingle.

STIR-BRAISED BROCCOLI OR CAULIFLOWER

2 bunches broccoli or 1 medium-large cauliflower
1 small onion
1 slice ginger root
1 clove garlic
3 Tb vegetable oil
salt and pepper to taste
4 Tb Vegetable Broth
2 Tb butter
3 Tb milk

Preparation
Break the broccoli or cauliflower into individual flowerets. Chop the onion into small pieces. Shred the ginger root. Crush the garlic.

Cooking
Heat the oil in a frying pan with a cover. When hot, add the onion, ginger, garlic, and salt and pepper to taste, and stir fry for 1 minute. Add the cauliflower and turn the pieces in the oil in a gentle stir fry for 2 minutes. Add Vegetable Broth, butter, and milk, and continue to stir fry gently for 2 minutes,

until the butter has melted and the liquid has coated the vegetable and is boiling vigorously. Reduce the heat to low, and cover the pan tightly. Allow the contents to simmer gently for 3–4 minutes. Remove cover, adjust for seasoning, turn the vegetable around gently a few times, and serve. In cooking broccoli, the simmering under cover may have to continue for a few minutes longer.

For nonvegetarians, break ½–1 chicken-stock cube over the vegetables when the broth, butter, and milk are added. In preparing more elaborate meals, a few tablespoons of Fu-Yung Sauce may be added before serving.

STIR-BRAISED BRUSSELS SPROUTS, CABBAGE, OR GREEN BEANS

　　1　lb brussels sprouts or 1 medium-size cabbage or ¾ lb green beans
　　2　slices ginger root
　　1　clove garlic
　　3　Tb vegetable oil
　　½　tsp salt
　　4　Tb Vegetable Broth
　　1½　Tb soy sauce
　　½　Tb hoisin sauce
　　2　Tb sherry
　　2　Tb butter
　　salt and pepper to taste

Preparation
Cut each sprout into halves or quarters, or trim ends of beans and cut them diagonally into 2-inch pieces, or remove the main stalk of the cabbage and slice it into 1-inch strips. Crush the ginger root and garlic.

Cooking
Heat the oil in a frying pan. Add salt, ginger, and garlic, stir a few times, and add the sprouts. Stir over medium heat for 2 minutes. Add the Vegetable Broth and stir fry gently for 2 minutes more. Add the soy sauce, hoisin sauce, sherry, and

butter. Turn the sprouts around two or three times. Cover the pan tightly. Reduce the heat to low, and allow the contents to simmer gently for 4–5 minutes. Remove cover, turn the vegetables around a few times, and adjust the seasoning. Serve in a bowl.

For nonvegetarians, break ¹/₂–1 chicken-stock cube over the vegetables when the broth is added. Or for increased flavor, 1 – 2 tablespoons Hot Black-Bean and Tomato or Hot Peanut-Butter Sauce may be added before serving.

STIR-BRAISED EGGPLANT OR ZUCCHINI

If cut into ¹/₃–¹/₂-inch-thick slices, these vegetables can be cooked in precisely the same manner as the sprouts or cabbage in the previous recipe. Hot Black-Bean and Tomato or Hot Peanut-Butter Sauce is also an effective addition to this dish.

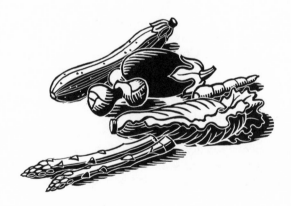

STIR-BRAISED CARROTS, ASPARAGUS, OR FRESH BAMBOO SHOOTS

The one quality that these three vegetables have in common is that they are crunchy and harder than any of the previous vegetables and therefore require somewhat longer cooking.

For them, the cooking order is frequently reversed: braising first, followed by stir frying. Sometimes they are parboiled, stir fried, braised, and finally stir fried once more.

1 lb young carrots or asparagus or bamboo shoots	½ cup Vegetable Broth
	1½ Tb soy sauce
	1 Tb hoisin sauce
1 clove garlic	2 Tb butter
3 Tb vegetable oil	1½ tsp sugar
1 slice ginger root	2 Tb sherry
1½ tsp salt	

Preparation
Trim the vegetable and slice diagonally into 1½–2-inch pieces. Crush the garlic.

Cooking
Parboil the vegetable in boiling water for 5–6 minutes. Drain thoroughly. Heat the oil in a frying pan. Add the ginger, garlic, and salt. Stir for ½ minute. Add the vegetables and stir fry gently over medium heat for 5 minutes. Pour in the Vegetable Broth, soy sauce, and hoisin sauce. Stir the contents a few times. Cover the pan tightly and leave the contents to simmer for 10–12 minutes. Remove cover, add the butter, sugar, and sherry, and raise the heat to high. Stir fry gently until the liquid in the pan is thick and has almost dried up. Serve immediately.

Asparagus, carrots, and bamboo shoots can all benefit from the addition of ½-dozen medium-sized Chinese dried mushrooms, which have been soaked in hot water for ½ hour, then cut into thin slices, and added along with the Vegetable Broth.

DEEP AND STIR FRY

This double method of cooking is often used in combining hard and semihard vegetables with soft vegetables in one dish. The hard and semihard vegetables are deep fried for a period, and then combined with the stir-fried soft vegetables.

The flavorers (seasonings and sauces) are not added until the second stage of the cooking. For instance, the hard vegetable in the preceding recipe—carrots, asparagus, or bamboo shoots—or turnips can be combined with Chinese cabbage and dried mushrooms very successfully in this way.

CASSEROLE OF DEEP-FRIED CARROTS, ASPARAGUS, AND BAMBOO SHOOTS AND QUICK-FRIED CHINESE CABBAGE AND MUSHROOMS

⅓ lb asparagus	2 tsp sesame oil
⅓ lb young carrots	½ tsp salt
⅓ lb bamboo shoots	2 Tb soy sauce
6 large Chinese dried mushrooms	1 Tb soy paste
	1 Tb hoisin sauce
½ lb Chinese or green cabbage	2 tsp sugar
	4 Tb Vegetable Broth
oil for deep frying	2 Tb sherry
2 Tb butter	

Preparation
Remove the coarse part of the asparagus and trim the carrots and bamboo shoots to the same thickness as the asparagus. Cut them into 1–2-inch segments. Soak the dried mushrooms for ½ hour in hot water and shred. Cut the cabbage into 1-inch slices.

Cooking
Place the carrots, asparagus, and bamboo shoots in a wire basket, and deep fry in hot oil for 6–7 minutes; drain thoroughly.

Meanwhile heat the butter and sesame oil in a casserole. When the butter has melted, add the mushrooms, stir for ½ minute, and add the cabbage and salt. Stir fry gently for 3–4 minutes over medium heat. Add the deep-fried vegetables and the flavorers, along with the Vegetable Broth and sherry. Raise the heat to high. Stir and turn the vegetables together for 3–4 minutes and serve in the casserole. Serves 4–6.

THE MONKS' MIXED VEGETABLE ENSEMBLE

This dish, which is widely enjoyed in China, can be prepared by repeating the previous recipe and adding three other items:

> 1 – 2 cakes bean curd
> ¼ lb cellophane noodles
> 2 oz lily-bud stems

Almost any other hard vegetable can be substituted for the asparagus or you can omit it; Chinese cooking is usually very flexible. You will also need to double the quantity of soy sauce (to 4 tablespoons) and use three times as much Vegetable Broth (12 tablespoons).

Cut the bean curd into 1-inch-square cubes and deep fry for 2 – 3 minutes, along with the other hard vegetables. Soak the cellophane noodles in hot water for 5 minutes and drain; cut the lily buds into 2-inch-long pieces and soak in 1 cup hot water for ½ hour together with the dried mushrooms (reserve the cup of water used for soaking these two ingredients). When the mushrooms, noodles, and lily buds are soft, add them with all the other vegetables to the casserole, together with the mushroom-and-lily-bud water. At this point the liquid may be thickened with 1 – 2 teaspoons cornstarch. The whole amalgam of vegetables should be allowed to cook gently for 10 minutes under cover in the casserole. Then sprinkle the vegetables with 1 – 2 tablespoons sherry and an extra 2 teaspoons sesame oil. The lily-bud stems contribute a distinctively Chinese musky flavor, which for Westerners is an acquired taste but reminds Chinese very much of the Good Earth and the Old Ancestral Country. Serves 4 – 6.

QUICK DEEP-FRIED AND STIR-FRIED MIXED VEGETABLES

If you have a deep fryer handy, you can combine the two methods of cooking in one quick process. As has been pointed out, in Chinese cooking, different methods are often combined or telescoped, not just to tenderize the food (which is, of course, part of it), but also to facilitate the amalgamation of flavors—flavors that sometimes arise only through the different cooking methods themselves.

¼ lb cabbage	1 Tb sesame oil
¼ lb bamboo shoots	1 tsp salt
⅓ lb spinach	¼ lb bean sprouts
2 cloves garlic	2 Tb soy sauce
2 slices ginger root	1 Tb hoisin sauce
oil for deep frying	4 Tb Vegetable Broth
2 Tb butter	2 Tb sherry

Preparation

Clean the cabbage and bamboo shoots and cut into 1½–2-inch pieces. Wash and dry the spinach, and remove the tougher stems. Crush the garlic and shred the ginger.

Cooking

Heat the oil in the deep fryer. When hot, place the cabbage and bamboo shoots in a wire basket and deep fry for 3 minutes. Drain. Heat the butter and sesame oil in a large frying pan. Add the salt, garlic, and ginger. Stir them around in the oil for ½ minute. Add the sprouts and spinach and stir fry over high heat for 2 minutes. Add all the other vegetables, soy sauce, hoisin sauce, and broth. Stir fry over high heat for 3 minutes. Sprinkle with sherry. For a full appreciation of the flavor, this dish should be eaten immediately. Serves 4–6.

QUICK DEEP-FRIED CAULIFLOWER (IN BATTER) WITH STIR-FRIED SEASONAL VEGETABLES

For seasonal vegetables, you can use ¼ pound bean sprouts, ¼ pound fresh mushrooms, and 2 ounces spring bamboo shoots. This recipe differs from the previous one in that the cauliflower (¼–½ pound) is deep fried in a light batter (consisting of 1 egg white, 2 tablespoons flour, and 4 tablespoons milk beaten for ¼ minute with a rotary beater). Break the cauliflower into 1½–2-inch flowerets. Dip it in the batter and deep fry for 3–4 minutes, then drain. Cut the mushrooms and bamboo shoots into very thin slices and stir fry in 4 tablespoons butter impregnated with small quantities of chopped garlic and onion for just a minute. Mix the two groups of vegetables together and stir fry. As in the previous recipe, all the various seasonings and flavorers are added to this final stir fry, which takes no more than 2–3 minutes over high heat. Because the cooking time is so short, the seasonal vegetables are very crisp, providing a contrast in surface texture to the vegetable cooked in batter, which is still crunchy inside. You may give the vegetable in batter a brief stir fry and add ½–1 teaspoon chili sauce, along with a little additional soy sauce, sugar, and oil, before combining with the other vegetables in the final stir fry. Serves 4–5.

QUICK DEEP-FRIED EGGPLANT AND/OR ZUCCHINI WITH STIR-FRIED SEASONAL VEGETABLES

Cut the eggplant and/or zucchini into 1–2-inch pieces. Dip them lightly in batter and then deep fry for 3–4 minutes. Drain. Follow with a very short period of stir frying in 1–2 tablespoons sesame oil and 1 teaspoon chili sauce. Then combine with the unbattered seasonal vegetables for the final stir fry together. Add the usual seasonings and flavorers: salt, soy sauce, hoisin sauce, Vegetable Broth, sugar, and sherry, after the seasonal vegetables have been treated to a minute's stir frying in 2 tablespoons butter. The same quantities of seasonings and flavorers can be used as in the recipe for Quick Deep-Fried and Stir-Fried Mixed Vegetables, if about ½ pound each eggplant and zucchini is to be cooked. The chili sauce adds a touch of liveliness to the dish. Serves 4–6.

QUICK DEEP-FRIED AND STIR-FRIED CHINESE OR SAVOY CABBAGE

When the vegetables are in season and particularly fresh, they can be cooked in this manner without any need to combine them with, or marry them to, other vegetables. When cooked on its own, the cabbage should be very fresh and tender. If savoy cabbage is used, only the tenderest parts of the hearts of the vegetable should be retained.

1 lb young Chinese cabbage or tender hearts of savoy cabbage	vegetable oil for deep frying
	2 Tb sesame oil for stir frying
½ Tb cornstarch blended in 3 Tb water	½ tsp salt
	pepper to taste
4 Tb Vegetable Broth	1½ Tb soy sauce
1 clove garlic	1½ tsp sugar
1 slice ginger root	2 Tb sherry

Preparation
Cut the cabbage across the stems into pieces 2–3 inches wide. In a bowl, blend the cornstarch-and-water mixture with the Vegetable Broth. Crush the garlic and ginger.

Cooking
Deep fry the cabbage in hot vegetable oil for 2 minutes and quickly drain. Heat the sesame oil in a frying pan. Add the ginger and garlic and stir fry for ½ minute over moderate heat. Add the cabbage and stir fry for 2 minutes. Add the salt, pepper, and soy sauce and stir fry together for 1 minute. Add the cornstarch-and-broth mixture, sugar, and sherry and continue to stir fry for 1½ minutes. As the vegetable here cooks largely on its own, with only the assistance of seasonings and flavorers, the appeal of the dish lies primarily in bringing out

the native taste and flavor of the vegetable itself, which often stands out for its purity amid the mixture of savoriness of a Chinese meal.

QUICK DEEP-FRIED AND STIR-FRIED SWEET-AND-SOUR CHINESE OR SAVOY CABBAGE

The difference between this dish and the previous one is that it does not require only the tenderest parts of the vegetable; much of the coarser leaves can be included. The procedure is exactly the same as in the preceding recipe, except that during the final stir fry, after all the seasonings and flavorers have been added, 5–6 tablespoons of Sweet-and-Sour Sauce are added, and the stir frying is extended for 1½–2 minutes. The extra cooking time helps both to tenderize the coarser parts of the vegetable and to give the sauce a chance to flavor and penetrate the vegetable. When the vegetables available are not of prime quality, this recipe is more suitable than the previous one.

QUICK DEEP-FRIED CELERY WITH STIR-FRIED RED PEPPER AND HOT-PICKLED SZECHUAN CABBAGE

Hot-pickled Szechuan cabbage resembles curry in that it is "hot" and therefore can blanket or camouflage most other flavors. But when used discreetly and in small quantities, it enhances and brings out the flavors of the other ingredients — meats as well as vegetables.

1 lb celery or broccoli	3 Tb Vegetable Broth
1 medium red sweet pepper	2 Tb soy sauce
1–2 oz hot-pickled Szechuan cabbage	1½ tsp sugar
	3 Tb Hot Black-Bean and Tomato Sauce
oil for deep frying	
2 Tb sesame oil or butter	

Preparation
Clean the celery or broccoli and cut diagonally into 2-inch pieces. Slice the sweet pepper into thin strips. Rinse the Szechuan cabbage and slice in the same manner.

Cooking
Place the celery or broccoli in a wire basket and deep fry in hot oil for 2 minutes; drain. Heat the sesame oil or butter in a large frying pan. When hot, add the sweet pepper and Szechuan cabbage. Stir fry quickly over high heat for 1½ minutes. Add the celery. Stir, toss, and mix the vegetables for 2 minutes. Add the Vegetable Broth, soy sauce, sugar, and Hot Black-Bean and Tomato Sauce. Stir, scramble, and toss for a further 2 minutes.

QUICK DEEP-FRIED AND STIR-FRIED GREEN BEANS

Since green beans are subtle in flavor, they are best cooked on their own rather than in combination with other vegetables.

1 lb young green beans	1 Tb hoisin sauce
2 cloves garlic	2 Tb Vegetable Broth
oil for deep frying	1½ Tb sherry
2 Tb butter	1 tsp sugar
1½ Tb soy sauce	

Preparation
Wash and dry the beans. Trim tops and bottoms if necessary. Crush the garlic.

Cooking
Heat the oil in the deep fryer. When very hot, place the beans in a wire basket. Deep fry the beans in two batches for 2 minutes and drain. Heat the butter in a frying pan. Add the garlic, soy sauce, hoisin sauce, and Vegetable Broth. Stir together over medium heat for 1 minute. Add the beans, turn the heat up to high. Add the sherry and sugar. Turn the beans around in the sauce for 2½ minutes. Serves 5 – 6.

QUICK DEEP-FRIED AND QUICK-FRIED BUTTON MUSHROOMS

This is a Yangchow dish, from the northern bank of the Yangtze.

1¼ lb button mushrooms	1 Tb salt
1 Tb cornstarch	1½ tsp freshly ground pepper
3 Tb Vegetable Broth	oil for deep frying
2 egg whites	2 Tb sesame oil or butter

Preparation
Remove the stems from the mushrooms. Wash and dry. Mix the cornstarch, Vegetable Broth, and egg whites together in a bowl. Beat for 10–15 seconds with a fork, until well blended. Dip the mushrooms into this batter. Heat and stir the salt and pepper in a small, very dry pan over low heat for 3 minutes until it develops a bouquet (this is Roasted Aromatic Salt-and-Pepper Mix).

Cooking
Heat the oil in the deep fryer. When hot, place the batter-covered mushrooms in a wire basket and deep fry for 2½ minutes; drain. Heat the sesame oil or butter in a frying pan. When hot, add the mushrooms, turn gently in the oil for 2 minutes. Leave to sauté for 2 minutes. Lightly sprinkle a pinch or two of the Aromatic Salt-and-Pepper Mix over the mushrooms. Serves 4–5.

PLAIN DEEP FRYING

Although in cooking vegetables deep frying is more often than not used in conjunction with other processes (as we have seen in the preceding recipes), it can sometimes be employed independently with success.

DEEP-FRIED MARINADED MUSHROOMS

1½ lb firm button mushrooms

For batter
2 eggs
½ cup plain flour
½ cup milk
oil for deep frying

For marinade
2 Tb soy sauce
½ Tb hoisin sauce
½ Tb yeast extract
1 Tb vinegar
1 Tb sherry
2 tsp sugar
1½ tsp chili sauce
2 Tb Vegetable Broth

Preparation
Clean the mushrooms thoroughly and remove the stems.
Beat the ingredients for the batter together with a rotary beater for 1 minute. Mix the ingredients for the marinade in a
bowl. Add the mushrooms to the marinade and let stand for 1
hour. Drain thoroughly.

Cooking
Dip each mushroom into the batter; drain off excess batter.
Place 4–5 mushrooms in a wire basket (or use a perforated
spoon) and deep fry for 3 minutes. Drain well. Repeat until
all the mushrooms have been deep fried.

Serving
The deep-fried mushrooms can be served as they are or with
any one of the following sauces:

MUSHROOM SAUCE

HOT BLACK-BEAN AND TOMATO SAUCE

FU-YUNG SAUCE

HOT PEANUT-BUTTER SAUCE

They can also be served with Roasted Aromatic Salt-and-
Pepper Mix. This should be used as a dip. Serves 4–6.

DEEP-FRIED MARINADED CAULIFLOWER, BROCCOLI, BAMBOO SHOOTS, ASPARAGUS, EGGPLANT, OR BRUSSELS SPROUTS

Any one of these vegetables can be treated in the same manner as the mushrooms in the previous recipe, but since they are harder vegetables, they require an extra minute of deep frying. Cooked in this way, and served with appropriate sauces or dips, they can be very welcome as starters (at a Western meal), or they can simply be served on their own as one of the several dishes in a multicourse or multidish Chinese meal. Because of their differing textures, they make an interesting accompaniment to stir-fried or clear-simmered dishes.

STEAMING

BECAUSE OF THE NATURE of Chinese cooking, one method is often combined with or overlaps another or several others. Only occasionally does one type of cooking stand entirely alone. Steaming is often employed in China either as an initial process, to soften tougher ingredients, or as a concluding one, to seal together the various ingredients. It may also be used as a single process, in cases where the cooking is best maintained at an even temperature, to avoid the risk of the dish drying up or becoming burned. Steaming is more widely used in China than in the West because the cooking of rice (usually in huge quantities) produces a great deal of steam, which can be utilized to help cook other parts of the meal.

Usually steaming is utilized to produce "pure" dishes, that is, dishes that do not contain much sauce or heavy seasoning but rely chiefly on the inherent flavor of the main ingredient. As food is generally steamed in the dishes in which it is served, the prepared dishes are customarily placed in a many-tiered bamboo steam basket over the cooking rice. To keep them hot, dishes are sometimes steamed just before they are brought to the table. Almost any dish cooked by another method can be steamed for a short period without losing any of its essential qualities. Hence a brief, brisk period of steaming to seal the dish is a common practice in China.

Longer periods of steaming in a covered vessel are usually reserved for "pudding" dishes—dishes that are packed into a large heatproof bowl, steamed for a prolonged period, then turned out onto a serving dish. This method is used more frequently for meat than for vegetables. Long steaming is equivalent to cooking in a double boiler. Dishes that are subjected to medium periods of steaming are usually "assembled" ones, in which foods that have been prepared, cooked, and flavored in different ways are combined in a heatproof bowl or a casserole, and then steamed together.

QUICK-STEAMED BUTTERED LETTUCE OR CHINESE CABBAGE

2–3 heads romaine lettuce or Chinese cabbage (about 1 lb)
1 tsp cornstarch blended in 2 Tb water
4 Tb Vegetable Broth
3 Tb butter
1 tsp salt
pepper to taste
1 Tb light soy sauce
1½ tsp sugar
2 Tb Guinness stout or 1 Tb sherry

Preparation
Remove the base and the coarser leaves of the vegetable. Cut the remaining leaves across the stem into 2–3-inch pieces. Blend the cornstarch mixture with the Vegetable Broth.

Cooking
Heat the butter in a large frying pan. When hot and melted, add the lettuce or cabbage. Spread it out, and stir and turn until it is well covered with the oil. Sprinkle with salt. Add the remaining ingredients. Turn and stir them together for ½ minute. Turn out onto a heatproof dish. Pour the gravy over it. Place the dish in a steamer and steam vigorously for 3–4 minutes. Serves 4–6.

QUICK-STEAMED BUTTERED SNOW PEAS

Snow peas can be cooked in precisely the same way as lettuce in the preceding recipe, except that in the final cooking the steaming can be continued for an extra minute. A clove of garlic and a slice of ginger may be added to the oil or butter in the initial frying stage to give just a touch of their flavor. They should be removed when the dish is served.

STEAMED BROCCOLI WITH FU-YUNG SAUCE

    1 lb broccoli
    1 clove garlic
    2 slices ginger root
    3 Tb vegetable oil
    1 tsp salt
    1 Tb butter
    4 Tb Vegetable Broth
    ½ Tb white bean-curd cheese
    1 Tb light soy sauce
    6 Tb Fu-Yung Sauce

Preparation
Cut the broccoli into 2–3-inch pieces or break into branches. Crush the garlic and shred the ginger.

Cooking
Heat the oil in a large frying pan. When hot, add the garlic and ginger and stir together for ½ minute. Add the broccoli, sprinkle with salt, and turn in the oil until every piece is well covered. Add the butter, Vegetable Broth, and bean-curd cheese. Stir fry all together for 2 minutes over medium heat. Spread the Fu-Yung Sauce over the broccoli, and empty the contents of the pan into a heatproof dish. Place the dish in a steamer and steam vigorously for 5–6 minutes. Serves 4–6.

Young leeks or cauliflower can be cooked in exactly the same manner.

For nonvegetarians, the Vegetable Broth can be replaced with 4 – 5 tablespoons concentrated chicken broth.

STEAMED CABBAGE WITH STEMS

To Chinese vegetarians, the hard stems of various vegetables are delicacies when they are properly prepared and cooked.

    1 medium-sized savoy cabbage
    1 stalk spring onion
    1 clove garlic
    2 slices ginger root
    2 tsp salt
    ¾ cup Vegetable Broth
    1 Tb yeast extract
    1½ tsp sugar
    2 Tb vegetable oil
    1 Tb butter
    1 Tb soy sauce
    1 Tb hoisin sauce

Preparation
Remove the leaves from the stems of the cabbage. Cut or carve the stems into neat bite-size pieces. Parboil for 3 – 4 minutes to remove any bitterness. Select the fresher leaves of the cabbage and slice into 2 – 3-inch pieces. Cut the spring onion into 1-inch lengths. Crush the garlic and ginger.

Cooking
Place the pieces of stem at the bottom of a large heatproof bowl. Sprinkle with 1 teaspoon salt. Pour in the Vegetable Broth and add the yeast extract and sugar. Cover the bowl with waxed paper, place in a steamer, and steam for 40 minutes.

Meanwhile heat the oil in a frying pan and add the ginger, garlic, and spring onion. Add the remaining 1 teaspoon salt and stir fry for ½ minute. Add the butter, cabbage, soy sauce, and hoisin sauce. Stir fry together for about 2 minutes, or until the vegetables are well covered with the oil and flavorers. Remove the waxed paper from the heatproof bowl and put the stir-fried vegetables on top of the ingredients in it. Steam vigorously for a further 4–5 minutes. Serve in the bowl. This dish is almost a soup; the diners will find the roots of the vegetable are at least as appealing as the freshly fried leaves (and to some, more satisfying). Serves 4–6.

PLAIN STEAMED CHINESE DRIED MUSHROOMS

This dish, another semisoup, is considered a delicacy and is, therefore, often served during a banquet, where its simplicity contrasts with the more elaborately prepared dishes.

20 selected Chinese dried mushrooms approximately even in size (⅓–½ lb)
2 stalks spring onion
1½ Tb light soy sauce
½ Tb yeast extract (optional)
½ tsp salt
1 tsp sugar
2 slices ginger root
2 cups Vegetable Broth

Preparation
Soak the mushrooms in 2 cups hot water for ½ hour. Remove the stems and discard. Cut the spring onions, including green parts, into 3–4-inch pieces.

Cooking
Put the mushrooms in a large heatproof glass bowl. Sprinkle with the soy sauce, yeast extract, salt, and sugar, and place the spring onion and ginger root on top. Pour in the Vegetable Broth. Tie a piece of waxed paper over the top of the bowl. Place the bowl in a steamer, and steam for 1 hour. Remove the ginger and spring onion. Steam for 10 minutes more. Serves 6–8.

STEAMED ZUCCHINI BOWL

1 very large zucchini (about 12 inches long)
4–5 large Chinese dried mushrooms
½ cup Chinese grass mushrooms or small button mushrooms
2 Tb gingko nuts or peanuts
1 cup Vegetable Broth
4 oz heart of cabbage
½ Tb yeast extract
1 Tb light soy sauce
2 tsp chopped red-in-snow
½ tsp salt
1 Tb butter
2 slices ginger root
2 Tb sherry

Preparation
Slice a 3-inch piece from the larger end of the zucchini to use as a lid, and set the remaining part firmly in a heatproof bowl. Scoop out the meat from the center, leaving a shell at least ½–¾-inch thick. Dice 6–7 ounces of this meat into ½–1-inch cubes. Soak the dried mushrooms for ½ hour and the grass mushrooms for ¼ hour in hot water. (Button mushrooms need not be soaked.) Discard the stems of the dried mushrooms and slice in thin strips. Boil the gingko nuts or peanuts for 10 minutes and drain. Heat the Vegetable Broth until it begins to boil.

Cooking
Place the zucchini cubes, grass mushrooms, gingko nuts, and heart of cabbage in the scooped-out cavity of the zucchini. Sprinkle with yeast extract, soy sauce, chopped red-in-snow, and salt. Pour in the boiling Vegetable Broth. Heat the butter in a frying pan. When hot, stir fry the sliced dried mushroom strips in it for 2 minutes. Place the mushroom strips on top of the other contents of the bowl. Add the 2 slices ginger. Close the Zucchini Bowl with the lid. Place it in a steamer, and steam for 1 hour. Add the sherry and steam for a further 3

minutes. Remove the 2 slices ginger and bring the bowl to the table, lifting the lid just before serving. Serves 6–8.

For nonvegetarians, use chicken stock instead of Vegetable Broth; a small amount of dried shrimp may be added with the other ingredients during the early stage of the cooking. Some fresh shrimp and cubes of diced chicken may be added along with the sherry.

STEAMED TURN-OUT VEGETABLE ENSEMBLE

Chinese "turn-out" dishes are cooked and served like puddings. They are cooked in deep heatproof bowls, and when ready to be served are turned out onto serving dishes. An assortment of vegetables and other ingredients is usually packed into the bowl, with the more piquant and stronger-tasting ones on top; this allows their flavor to percolate through the bowl in the course of the cooking. Any excess of stock or gravy is absorbed by the transparent cellophane noodles, which are great absorbers of liquid but never become soft and mushy however long they are cooked.

¼–½ lb selected stems of cabbage
¼–½ lb broccoli and cauliflower
2 Tb butter
4 oz cellophane noodles
3 oz button mushrooms or 6 large Chinese dried mushrooms
2 Tb light soy sauce
2 zucchini
1 medium-sized eggplant
1 cake bean curd
oil for deep frying
½ tsp salt
pepper to taste
1 Tb hoisin sauce
½ Tb bean-curd cheese
2 Tb sherry
2 Tb red-in-snow
1 cup Vegetable Broth

Preparation

Cut the stems of the cabbage into 1–1½-inch pieces, discarding any unsightly parts. Break the cauliflower and broccoli into individual flowerets and branches. Rub the inside of a large heatproof bowl with butter, and press the pieces of cabbage, cauliflower, and broccoli against the sides of the bowl. Soak the cellophane noodles in warm water for 5 minutes. Drain, mix them with the button mushrooms (or dried mushrooms, which have been soaked for ½ hour in hot water), and pour into the bowl. Over this sprinkle 2 tablespoons soy sauce. Slice the zucchini and eggplant into ½-inch-thick slices, and the bean-curd cake into 8 pieces. Place in a wire basket and deep fry in oil together for 3 minutes. Drain and place on top of the noodles. Sprinkle the contents with salt, pepper, hoisin sauce, bean-curd cheese, sherry, and finely chopped red-in-snow. Finally pour in the Vegetable Broth.

Cooking

Tie a sheet of waxed paper or aluminum foil over the top of the bowl. Place the bowl in a steamer and steam steadily for 1 hour. By this time all the liquid in the bowl should have been absorbed by the noodles.

Serving

Remove the waxed paper or foil. Turn the contents of the bowl onto a well-heated deep-sided dish and serve. The steaming mound of mixed vegetables is a most appetizing sight. Serves 6–8.

STEAMED BEAN CURD WITH PEANUT-BUTTER SAUCE

2 cakes bean curd	1 Tb vinegar
3 Tb peanut butter or	1 tsp chili sauce
sesame paste	2 Tb sherry
3 Tb sesame oil	1 tsp sugar
3 Tb soy sauce	

Preparation and Cooking

Cut each piece of bean-curd cake into 8 pieces, and place in a heatproof dish. Place the dish in the steamer and steam vigorously for 10 minutes. Heat all the other ingredients in a small saucepan over gentle heat, stirring continuously for 2½ minutes. Pour the hot sauce evenly over the bean curds. Serves 4 – 5.

STEAMED PARSNIPS AND CARROTS IN HOT PEANUT-BUTTER SAUCE

³/₄ lb young carrots
³/₄ lb baby parsnips
2 sprigs parsley
3 Tb butter

For sauce
3 Tb peanut butter or 2 Tb sesame paste
2 Tb sesame oil
2 Tb soy sauce
2 tsp sugar
2 tsp chili sauce or 1 tsp Chinese chili oil
2 Tb sherry
1 Tb tomato purée
2 Tb Vegetable Broth

Preparation
Trim and scrape the carrots and parsnips. Cut diagonally into 2 – 3-inch pieces. Chop the parsley finely. Mix the sauce mixture in a small heavy saucepan.

Cooking
Heat the butter in a frying pan. When it has melted, turn the carrots and parsnips in the butter a few times and transfer to a large open heatproof dish. Place the dish in a steamer and steam for 45 minutes.

Meanwhile, heat the sauce mixture gently over low heat. Stir continuously for 2½ minutes, until the ingredients are well blended.

Serving
Pour the sauce evenly over the carrots and parsnips, sprinkle with parsley. Serves 5 – 6.

STEAMED GREEN BEANS IN HOT PEANUT-BUTTER SAUCE

Green beans can be prepared in the same manner as the carrots and parsnips in the previous recipe: turn them in butter, steam them for 30 minutes. The quantities of ingredients for the Hot Peanut-Butter Sauce should be reduced by about 1/3, but the procedure is otherwise the same. No parsley is required for green beans.

HOT MARINADING

HOT-MARINADING (*lu*) is a cooking process that may well be peculiar to the Chinese. It consists of marinading or heating the ingredients in a Master Sauce or master marinade for a period of time, and then preparing them for serving—slicing them into suitably sized pieces; or cooking them quickly by stir frying, deep frying, roasting, grilling, or steaming; or combining them with other foods that have been prepared and cooked in other ways. Quite often foods that have been hot marinaded—especially meats—are simply left to cool and then sliced and served cold. Many items of the Chinese hors d'oeuvre are prepared in this manner. Hot-marinaded vegetables are usually quickly stir fried or deep fried before serving to give them a final sealing of ingredients. Without this final sealing, vegetables that have been merely boiled are liable to be insipid. Although vegetables that have been hot marinaded in a Master Sauce are vastly superior in taste to vegetables that have been boiled, a brisk dip in hot oil—even in a small quantity of oil—together with some final adjustments in flavor and aromatic ingredients, often improves their taste immeasurably. Since hot marinading is a comparatively slow process, it allows harder vegetables time to cook through and tenderize before being mixed with softer vegetables for a short period of stir frying.

The roots or stems of the vegetables may be cut up and hot marinaded before they are reunited with their leaves during stir frying. Thus hot marinading, like other Chinese methods of cooking, can be employed as a single process on its own, but it is more often used in conjunction with other processes. And here too one method runs into another. In Chinese cooking, it is through marriage and intermarriage, or even remarriage, that the best results are achieved!

MASTER SAUCE

The Master Sauce used in hot marinading is made from familiar ingredients: soy sauce, soybean paste, sherry, sugar, salt, onion, ginger root, anise, five-spice powder, peppercorns, and the foods that have been cooked in the Master Sauce. If five-spice powder and anise are difficult to obtain, 1 – 2 bags (or tablespoons) bouquet garni can be substituted.

In vegetarian cooking, the Master Sauce is best started by cooking two or more batches of hard vegetables in the flavorers, with one batch of semihard vegetables, one after another, such as carrots, wax beans, and turnips with eggplant (the carrots, beans, and turnips for 45 minutes, and the eggplant for 25 minutes), or carrots and corn or dried beans with green beans (the first 2 vegetables for 40 minutes, and the green beans for 25 minutes). The vegetarian Master Sauce is less stable than the nonvegetarian variety as more water is released by the vegetables during cooking. To keep it "alive," it is best to use it at least twice a week; it should be well strained through cheesecloth and skimmed after each cooking. It should always be kept in the refrigerator.

For nonvegetarians, the Master Sauce is usually begun by making a red-cooked dish of chicken, duck, beef, lamb, or pork. A panful of sauce is brought to a boil, and large pieces of meat, or whole birds, are simmered slowly in it for 1 hour or more. The meat or poultry is then removed for serving and the sauce reserved for further use. The more the foods that have been cooked in the sauce, the richer and more complex it becomes and the better it is as a base for further cooking.

After each cooking, the sauce should be skimmed and strained. The sauce is kept "alive" by cooking fresh materials in it at least once a week; between times it should be kept in the refrigerator.

The following are the quantities for 1 quart vegetarian Master Sauce:

  ¼ lb dried beans
  ¼ lb carrots
  ¼ lb turnips
  3 oz dried mushrooms
  1 cup water
  4 medium-size onions
  2 cloves garlic
  3 cups Vegetable Broth
  1 cup soy sauce
  ½ cup dry sherry
  2 Tb hoisin sauce
  2 Tb soybean paste
  3 Tb sugar
  6 slices ginger root
  2 bags or 2 Tb bouquet garni, or ⅓ tsp five-spice powder
    and ¼ tsp ground peppercorn
  ¼ lb green beans (optional)
  ¼ lb peanuts

Preparation

Soak dried beans overnight and drain. Scrape and clean the carrots and turnips. Cut diagonally into 2-inch pieces. Soak the dried mushrooms for ½ hour in 1 cup water. Slice the onions. Crush the garlic.

Cooking

Place the liquids (including mushroom water), onions, garlic, soybean paste, sugar, ginger, and bouquet garni in a heavy pan and bring to the boil. Add the dried beans, mushrooms, carrots, turnips, green beans, and peanuts, and simmer very gently for 1½ hours. Remove the vegetables, and strain the Master Sauce through cheesecloth. It is now ready for use. When using the sauce for hot marinading, place an asbestos pad under the pan so that it is kept at a very slow simmer.

In cooking, enough Master Sauce should be used to submerge the vegetables completely. As a general rule, this will mean about 3 cups sauce for 1 pound vegetables. The thrifty need not worry if this involves a large quantity of sauce, since it can be reused and therefore will not go to waste.

HOT-MARINADED STIR-FRIED GREEN BEANS

> 3/4 lb green beans
> Master Sauce
> 1 clove garlic
> 2 Tb butter
> 1 Tb sherry

Preparation and Cooking
Hot marinade the beans for 1/2 hour in Master Sauce to cover. Crush the garlic. Melt the butter in a frying pan over medium heat and add the garlic. Turn and stir a few times. Drain the beans well, add to the frying pan, and stir fry for 1 1/2 minutes. Add the sherry and continue to stir fry for another minute before serving. Serves 4 – 5.

HOT-MARINADED CARROTS AND TURNIPS

> 3/4 lb carrots
> 1/4 lb turnips
> Master Sauce
> 3 Tb butter
> 2 Tb sherry
> 2 Tb chopped parsley

Preparation and Cooking
Dice the carrots and turnips and simmer in Master Sauce to cover. Drain well. Heat the butter in a frying pan over low heat. Add the carrots and turnips. Turn the vegetables in the butter for 2 minutes. Add the sherry and continue to turn and stir gently for 1 minute more. Sprinkle with parsley. Serves 4 – 5.

HOT MARINADED CELERY STIR FRIED WITH CHINESE DRIED MUSHROOMS

1 lb celery
4 oz Chinese dried mushrooms
½ Tb cornstarch blended in 2 Tb Vegetable Broth
1 Tb sherry
Master Sauce
3 Tb butter

Preparation

Clean the celery thoroughly. Slice diagonally into 2-inch lengths. Soak the mushrooms in hot water for ½ hour. Reserve 3–4 tablespoons mushroom water. Remove mushroom stems. Slice caps into thin strips. Blend the mushroom water with the cornstarch mixture and sherry.

Cooking

Bring the Master Sauce to the boil and simmer the celery in it for 10 minutes. Remove and drain. Heat the butter in a frying pan over medium heat. Add the mushrooms to stir fry for 2 minutes. Add the hot-marinaded celery. Stir fry together over high heat for 2 minutes. Pour in the cornstarch mixture blended with the mushroom water and sherry. Turn and stir a few times. Serve as soon as the gravy has thickened. Serves 4–5.

HOT-MARINADED DEEP-FRIED EGGPLANT OR ASPARAGUS TIPS WITH NOODLES AND SLICED CUCUMBER

In this dish the hot-marinaded, deep-fried eggplant or asparagus tips provide a richness that is perfectly counterbalanced by the freshness of the watercress and cucumber.

3/4 lb eggplant or asparagus
4-inch piece cucumber
3 oz cellophane noodles
Master Sauce
vegetable oil for deep frying
4 Tb butter
1/2 tsp salt
1 Tb light soy sauce
1/2 cup Vegetable Broth
2 tsp sesame oil
1 Tb chopped watercress

Preparation
Cut the eggplant into slices 1/2-inch thick. Peel the cucumber, cut in two, and slice into matchsticks. Soak the noodles in warm water for 1/4 hour and drain.

Cooking
Simmer the eggplant in Master Sauce to cover for 10 minutes and drain. Deep fry in the vegetable oil for 3 minutes and drain. Heat the butter in a large frying pan. When melted, add the cucumber and stir fry over medium heat for 1 minute. Add the noodles. Turn them together over low heat for 2 minutes. Add the salt and soy sauce. Pour in the Vegetable Broth. Allow to cook over medium heat for 2 minutes. Add the deep-fried eggplant. Turn the pieces over among the noodles and cucumber a few times. Sprinkle with sesame oil and chopped watercress and serve in a large bowl. Serves 4–6.

HOT-MARINADED DEEP-FRIED VEGETABLE STEAK WITH STIR-FRIED SPINACH

3 pieces or about ½ lb vegetable steak	Master Sauce
	2 Tb vegetable oil
¾ lb spinach	2 Tb butter
2 cloves garlic	2 Tb soy sauce
2 slices ginger root	2 Tb sherry
oil for deep frying	4 Tb Vegetable Broth

Preparation
Vegetable steak is a high-protein soybean product available in cans from health-food stores. Cut each "steak" into 4 pieces. Wash and dry the spinach thoroughly, and remove some of the tougher stems. Crush the garlic and ginger.

Cooking
Simmer the pieces of "steak" in Master Sauce for 10 minutes. Deep fry in hot oil for 3 minutes. Drain and keep hot. Heat the vegetable oil in a large frying pan or saucepan. Add the garlic and ginger. Stir fry over high heat for ½ minute. Add the spinach and butter. Stir fry in the oil for 3 minutes. Add the soy sauce and sherry. Continue to stir fry over high heat for 2 minutes. With a perforated spoon, lift the spinach onto a serving dish. Place the "steaks" on top of the spinach. Add the broth to the frying pan, stir, and pour the gravy in the frying pan over the "steaks." Serves 4 – 5.

MIXED-FRIED HOT-MARINADED VEGETABLES WITH HOT PEANUT-BUTTER SAUCE

The people of Fukien Province like to use sesame paste or peanut-butter sauce in their stir-fried cooking, for both meat and vegetable dishes. This is one of their more aromatic vegetable dishes.

½ lb broccoli
½ lb asparagus tips
½ lb young carrots
   or zucchini
2 cloves garlic
Master Sauce

2 Tb vegetable oil
2 tsp sesame oil
1 slice ginger root
4 Tb Hot Peanut-Butter Sauce
2 Tb sherry

Preparation

Break the broccoli into 2–3-inch pieces; discard the coarser stems. Cut the asparagus into 2–3-inch segments. Scrape the carrots or zucchini and cut diagonally into 1–2-inch pieces. Crush the garlic.

Cooking

Simmer the carrots in the Master Sauce for 20 minutes; add the asparagus and broccoli (or zucchini, if used) and simmer for another 10 minutes. Strain. Heat the sesame oil in a frying pan. Add the ginger and garlic. Stir fry over medium heat for ½ minute. Add the vegetables and Hot Peanut-Butter Sauce, and stir fry together for 1½ minutes. Add the sherry. Continue to stir fry for ½ minute. Serves 4–6.

HOT-MARINADED BEAN-CURD STICKS WITH QUICK-FRIED BEAN SPROUTS

Bean-curd sticks are the dried skin of bean curd. They are pale beige in color and have a shiny surface.

6 oz bean-curd sticks
2 stalks spring onion
Master Sauce
4 Tb vegetable oil
¾ lb bean sprouts
½ tsp salt

1 Tb soy sauce
1 Tb hoisin sauce
1 tsp yellow bean-curd
   cheese
3 Tb Vegetable Broth

Preparation

Soak the bean-curd sticks in warm water for 2 hours. Cut into 2–3-inch segments. Chop the spring onions finely.

Cooking

Simmer the bean-curd sticks in the Master Sauce for 30 minutes, and drain. Heat 3 tablespoons vegetable oil in a large saucepan over a high heat. Add the bean sprouts, sprinkle with salt, and stir fry quickly for 2 minutes. Add the remaining 1 tablespoon oil to the middle of the pan, scooping and pushing the bean sprouts to the sides. Add soy sauce, hoisin sauce, and bean-curd cheese to the oil, and mix quickly. Add the Vegetable Broth. As it boils rapidly, stir and turn the bean sprouts. Add the bean-curd sticks. Stir fry them together with the bean sprouts for 2 minutes. Turn onto a serving dish. Sprinkle with chopped spring onion. Serves 5–6.

HOT-MARINADED CABBAGE WITH SWEET-AND-SOUR SAUCE

1½ lb cabbage (savoy if available)
Master Sauce
4 Tb vegetable oil
1 tsp salt
½ cup Sweet-and-Sour Sauce

Preparation and Cooking

Cut the cabbage against the stem into 1½-inch slices. Simmer it in the Master Sauce for 7–8 minutes, and drain. Heat the oil in a large frying pan. When hot, add the cabbage, sprinkle with salt, and stir fry over high heat for 3 minutes. Pour in the Sweet-and-Sour Sauce. Stir and blend gently. Serve as soon as the sauce thickens and becomes translucent. Serves 4–6.

HOT-MARINADED SHREDDED CARROTS WITH SHREDDED RADISH AND HOT-PICKLED SZECHUAN CABBAGE

    1 lb carrots
    4 oz radishes
    2 oz hot-pickled Szechuan cabbage
    Master Sauce
    3 Tb vegetable oil
    1 Tb sesame oil
    3 Tb Vegetable Broth
    1 Tb chopped coriander leaves

Preparation

Trim ends of carrots and radishes, then scrape and rinse. Slice into strips about ¼ inch wide. Cut Szechuan hot-pickled cabbage into similar size pieces.

Cooking

Simmer the carrots in the Master Sauce for 15 minutes, and drain. Heat the vegetable oil in a large frying pan. When hot, add the radishes and Szechuan cabbage, and stir fry together over high heat for 2 minutes. Add the carrots and stir fry together for 3 minutes. Add the sesame oil and Vegetable Broth, and stir fry 3 minutes longer. Sprinkle with chopped coriander leaves. Serves 4 – 6.

BOILING AND STEWING

BOILING is seldom used to cook vegetables in China—except for parboiling, which is intended solely for tenderizing hard vegetables. And vegetables can be equally well tenderized by sautéing, braising, deep frying, or slow cooking in broth, etc. These methods permit greater retention of flavor, because they avoid immersing the vegetables, which have a high water content, in an even greater quantity of water—as is the case in boiling. To add water to water, or to cook water in water, is hardly a promising route to tasty cooking, and yet it is the one most widely used in this country!

Parboiling is, however, often used in Chinese cooking, mainly because stir frying—the method of cooking most frequently used in China—is often a very short process, lasting a minute or two or sometimes less, and some pretenderizing of food is often necessary to prepare it for the rapid pace of flavoring and tenderizing during the final stage of cooking. In China, much parboiling is done in broth, so that as the meats or vegetables are tenderized, their flavors are also intensified. Usually only a small quantity of broth is required. The vegetables do not have to be drowned; they need only be turned in broth, with the broth meanwhile constantly reducing. When the broth evaporates during cooking, and when more and other types of food are added to the pot, the process is very much like stewing. When the precooked materials, which have been cooked and prepared in different ways — deep frying, parboiling, braising, etc. — are assembled together in a short process of stewing, we have what we call *hui,* or hot assembly.

Chinese stewing is precisely the same as the Western method, except that in Chinese stewing we usually add some soy sauce or soybean paste, or both, and chopped or shredded ginger and sugar to enhance the flavor (apart from the usual seasonings). In hot assembly at least one ingredient, usually cut-up bean-curd cakes, has been deep fried beforehand, and very often a drop or two of sesame oil is added at the last moment of cooking for an earthy, aromatic effect. It is the nature of stews that they are seldom pure dishes containing only one vegetable; generally they are an assembly of several vegetables and other ingredients, conforming to the Chinese concept of the orchestration of flavors. However, a number of dishes involving only a single vegetable are extremely successful and easily achieved.

RED-COOKED VEGETABLES

Typical of these one-vegetable dishes are the so-called red-cooked dishes, which means that they are cooked or stewed with soy sauce. Indeed, almost any food can be red cooked.

RED-COOKED EGGPLANT

1 1/2 lb eggplant	3 Tb soy sauce
1/2 lb tomatoes	1/2 cup Vegetable Broth
2 cloves garlic	1 Tb butter
2 slices ginger root	pepper to taste
3 Tb vegetable oil	3 Tb red wine
1/2 tsp salt	1 1/2 tsp sesame oil
1 tsp sugar	

Preparation
Cut the eggplant into 2½-by-1½-inch pieces. Skin the tomatoes and cut into quarters. Crush the garlic and shred the ginger.

Cooking
Heat the vegetable oil in a casserole. Add the garlic and ginger, and stir fry for ½ minute. Add the eggplant, and turn the pieces in the oil for 2 minutes over high heat. Add the tomatoes. Sprinkle the contents of the casserole with salt, sugar, and soy sauce, and pour in the Vegetable Broth. Turn the contents over a couple of times. Reduce the heat to low, cover, and cook for 15 minutes. Remove cover. Add the butter, pepper, wine, and sesame oil. Turn the contents gently and cook 5 minutes longer. Serves 4–6.

For nonvegetarians, omit the salt and add ½–1 chicken-stock cube, 4–5 tablespoons red-cooked meat gravy—from red-cooked meat—and 1 tablespoon dried shrimps at the beginning of the stewing. Use chicken broth or good meat stock instead of Vegetable Broth in the cooking.

RED-COOKED BROCCOLI OR BRUSSELS SPROUTS

Broccoli and brussels sprouts can be prepared in precisely the same manner as the eggplant in the previous recipe, except that the cooking time can be reduced from 15 to 10 minutes, and the tomato can be omitted. The broccoli should be broken into individual branches about 2 inches long, and the sprouts should each be cut into quarters, before they are fried. Serves 4–6.

For nonvegetarians, use good meat or chicken stock instead of vegetarian broth, add a few tablespoons of red-cooked meat gravy, and ½–1 chicken-stock cube. These should enhance the "meaty" flavor of the vegetables considerably.

RED-COOKED CABBAGE

This method produces one of the most popular and successful of red-cooked vegetable dishes. Indeed even meat eaters
sometimes choose it in preference to a meat dish. Although it
is prepared and cooked in much the same way as other red-
cooked vegetable dishes, this is a Chinese "classic" — as well
as a very useful dish in any context — so it is justifiable to
spell out the details again.

1 – 2 cloves garlic	2 Tb butter
1 – 2 slices ginger root	3 Tb soy sauce
(optional)	½ tsp salt
1 medium onion	1 tsp sugar
1½ – 2 lb savoy or	½ cup Vegetable Broth
Chinese cabbage	pepper to taste
3 Tb vegetable oil	2 – 3 Tb red wine or sherry

Preparation
Crush the garlic, shred the ginger, and cut the onion into
thin slices. Cut the cabbage into strips 1 inch thick. Remove
the root and cut each strip into quarters.

Cooking
Heat the oil and melt the butter in a heavy saucepan or casserole. Add the garlic, ginger, and onion, and stir fry for 1 minute. Add the cabbage and turn it in the oil for 2 minutes, until it is completely covered. Add the soy sauce, salt, sugar,
Vegetable Broth, and pepper. Turn the contents over a few
times. Reduce the heat to low (insert an asbestos pad under
the pan, if available), cover, and cook for 10 – 12 minutes.
Pour in the wine or sherry. Turn the contents over a couple
of times. Serves 4 – 6.

Celery, celeriac, or red cabbage can be red-cooked in the
same manner as cabbage and with equal success. Cauliflower
is usually white cooked rather than red cooked (see next section).

*For nonvegetarians, omit the salt, and add ½ – 1 chicken-
stock cube, 3 – 4 tablespoons red-cooked meat gravy, and 2 tea-*

spoons dried shrimp at the beginning of the stewing. Use chicken broth or good meat stock instead of Vegetable Broth.

RED-COOKED CARROTS AND/OR TURNIPS

Carrots can be red cooked in the same manner as any of the previous vegetables, but they require a much longer cooking time — 30 – 40 minutes — as do turnips cooked in this way.

When carrots and turnips are cooked in this manner, they should be cut into triangular wedges (of about 1½ inches), and since they require about the same length of time in cooking, they can mix in the same pot, thus providing some contrast in color, texture, and taste.

The important point about cooking these two vegetables is that after the initial stir frying over high heat, they should be covered and simmered over very low heat for the rest of the cooking period. They should be turned over once every 15 – 20 minutes to ensure even cooking. Alternatively, they can be cooked in a casserole placed in an oven at 300 degrees for 1 hour.

For nonvegetarians, omit the salt, and add ½ – 1 chicken-stock cube, 3 – 4 tablespoons red-cooked meat gravy, and 2 teaspoons dried shrimp at the stewing stage. Use chicken broth or good stock instead of Vegetable Broth. In China, the favorite meat to cook with turnips is beef. In that case, the best meat gravy to use would be red-cooked beef gravy and ½ – 1 beef-stock cube, in addition to the other ingredients.

RED-COOKED DRIED KIDNEY OR WAX BEANS AND CHESTNUTS

All these items can be red cooked, but they are seldom served on their own. Dried beans must be soaked overnight, and both dried beans and chestnuts need to be parboiled for 20 minutes before being added to red cook with the other items. They may be added to carrots and turnips, but much more often chestnuts are cooked together with red-cooked pork or beef. Beans of this type, which require a very long cooking period (1½ hours or more), are usually fried in oil and added to the pot before all the other ingredients. They may later be combined with bean-curd cakes (quickly deep fried), cellophane noodles, and a host of other vegetables — such as mushrooms, peas, cauliflower, leeks, etc. — which require 10–12 minutes or less to cook. The beans are red cooked first, and the other ingredients are prepared while the beans continue cooking slowly. They are then all assembled to cook together. Here we approach the assembled dishes, where a small amount of bean-curd cheese (red or white) and sesame oil are often added to enhance flavor and aroma.

WHITE-COOKED VEGETABLES

As previously mentioned, white cooking simply means cooking without the soy sauce or soybean paste. Because these last two soybean products are used universally as the general flavorers in Chinese cooking, their significance and importance cannot be overestimated. When they are omitted, a sort of vacuum is created that must be filled. In nonvegetarian cooking, this is done by the use of concentrated chicken broth or meat stock, supplemented by such items as dried shrimp, dried mussels and oysters, or shrimp sauce.

In vegetarian cooking, the vacuum is filled largely by the use of stronger vegetarian broth (obtained by simmering a greater quantity of dried beans in preparing it), light soy sauce supplemented by white bean-curd cheese, dried light-colored mushrooms, commercial mushroom sauce, and ingredients such as bean curds that have been deep fried for a short time in sesame oil. Foods with distinctive flavors, such as lily-bud stems, as well as pickled and salted items, may be added. The stronger spices, such as pepper, curry, chili, and mustard are also more frequently employed than in nonvegetarian cooking. In the West, milk and cream can also be used.

One of the most common white-cooked dishes is:

WHITE-COOKED CABBAGE

1 – 2 cloves garlic	½ tsp salt
1 – 2 slices ginger root	1 tsp sugar
1 medium onion	1 Tb white bean-curd cheese
1½ – 2 lb cabbage	2 Tb light soy sauce
½ cup Enriched Vegetable Broth (made from 2½ lb dried beans)	4 Tb cream
	2 Tb white wine
	2 tsp sesame oil
3 Tb vegetable oil	freshly ground pepper to taste
2 Tb butter	

Preparation

Crush the garlic, shred the ginger, and slice the onion very thinly. Cut the cabbage into ½-inch-thick slices.

To prepare the Enriched Vegetable Broth soak 2½ pounds dried beans overnight. Simmer very slowly in 6 cups water in a covered saucepan for 3 – 3½ hours, or cook in a casserole in the oven at 300 – 325 degrees for 3 hours. The same result can be achieved using a pressure cooker, in 30 – 35 minutes. Add the resultant reduced liquid to ordinary Vegetable Broth, 2 parts liquid to 3 parts broth.

Cooking

Heat the vegetable oil in a saucepan, add garlic, ginger, and onion, and stir fry together over medium heat for 1 minute. Add the cabbage and butter, and turn the vegetables until all the butter has melted and the vegetable pieces are coated with oil. Add the salt, sugar, bean-curd cheese, light soy sauce, Enriched Vegetable Broth, and cream. Turn the contents several times, cover, and cook gently for 12 – 15 minutes. Remove cover, add the wine and sesame oil, and sprinkle the contents with freshly ground pepper. Turn the vegetables over a couple of times. Serves 6 – 8.

For nonvegetarians, use chicken broth instead of Vegetable Broth and a chicken-stock cube instead of salt.

WHITE-COOKED CELERY

Repeat the previous recipe, using celery instead of cabbage.
Serves 4–6.

WHITE-COOKED CAULIFLOWER

Cauliflower can be white cooked in precisely the same manner as the celery and cabbage in the preceding recipes. With
cauliflower a white Fu-Yung Sauce is often poured over the
vegetable just before serving. As cauliflower will break into
unattractive bits if it is stirred with too great vigor (unlike
cabbage and celery, which can be roughly treated without any
ill effects), it is often somewhat undercooked (over heat for
only 5–6 minutes), and then steamed for another 3–4 minutes
in a heatproof dish in which it has been carefully arranged,
with the white Fu-Yung Sauce carefully poured over.

White cooking is applicable to a majority of vegetables that
require cooking for only 10–20 minutes. It can, therefore, be
used with good effect with broccoli, brussels sprouts, green
beans, cabbage, and zucchini, but is not often used with
eggplant (which has too red a color and is more suitable to
red cooking) or with vegetables such as carrots, turnips, and
chestnuts, which require a good deal longer cooking and are
consequently also best red cooked. It is never used with
quick-cooked leafy vegetables, such as spinach, bean sprouts,
lettuce, or watercress, or with sliced cucumber; these are best
stir fried in oil or butter, with as little liquid as possible added so that they can maintain their crisp-crunchy quality
when served. Cooking in liquid will cause them to wilt.

WHITE-COOKED BROCCOLI, BRUSSELS SPROUTS, GREEN BEANS, OR ZUCCHINI

All these vegetables can be white cooked in the same manner
as cauliflower: that is, stir fried for a short period and cooked
for 5–6 minutes, covered, along with the same ingredients

as for cabbage or cauliflower. Zucchini must of course be cut into suitable slices or wedges first. Like cauliflower, it is often best steamed for 3–4 minutes with Fu-Yung Sauce poured over it just before serving.

These last touches enhance the tenderness and color of the vegetables. Sometimes pickled or salted vegetables, such as red-in-snow, are finely chopped and sprinkled over the plain white-cooked vegetables to give them added interest.

WHITE-COOKED BAMBOO SHOOTS WITH CHINESE MUSHROOMS

1 clove garlic	³⁄₄ Tb white bean-curd
1 slice ginger root	cheese
1 8–10-oz can bamboo	½ cup Enriched Vegetable
shoots	Broth
3–4 oz Chinese dried	1½ Tb butter
mushrooms	2 oz green peas
2 Tb vegetable oil	1 Tb white wine or sherry
2 Tb light soy sauce	1 tsp sesame oil

Preparation
Crush the garlic and shred the ginger. Cut the bamboo shoots into 1-inch-by-½-inch wedges. Soak the mushrooms in hot water for ½ an hour. Remove the stems and cut each mushroom into quarters.

Cooking
Heat the vegetable oil in a heavy saucepan or casserole. Add the garlic and ginger, and stir fry over medium heat for ½ minute. Add the bamboo shoots. Continue to stir fry for 2–3 minutes. Add the soy sauce, bean-curd cheese, and Enriched Vegetable Broth. Cover and cook over low heat for 15 minutes. Add the butter, mushrooms, and peas. Turn the contents over 3–4 times and continue to cook over low heat for 5 minutes. Add the wine and sesame oil. Stir the contents around a few times.

HOT ASSEMBLY

In this form of stewing, several kinds of vegetables, prepared in different ways, are combined in one pot and cooked for a short while before serving (in a large bowl or tureen or in the cooking pot or casserole itself). The marrying of one material with another makes it similar to stir frying, but in stir frying the ingredients are fried together, while in hot assembly previously cooked ingredients are heated or stewed together for a short period. Two of the ingredients most commonly used in hot assembly are bean-curd cakes (*tofu*) and cellophane noodles, which, because they absorb a great deal of the gravy or soup in the dish, as well as the flavors of all the other ingredients, link together the many different items — and contribute added body.

THE LO-HAN DISH OF THE MONKS' MIXED VEGETABLES

2 cakes bean curd	2 cloves garlic
oil for deep frying	1 medium onion
4 oz cellophane noodles	2 Tb vegetable oil
3 oz Chinese dried	3 Tb butter
mushrooms	1/2 tsp salt
1 oz wood ears	21/2 Tb soy sauce
3 oz dried bamboo shoots	1/2 Tb red bean-curd cheese
2 lily-bud stems	1 tsp sugar
1/2 lb cabbage	pepper to taste
1/2 lb broccoli	11/2 cups Vegetable Broth
1/4 lb celery	2 Tb dry sherry
1/4 lb green beans	2 tsp sesame oil
1/4 lb eggplant	

Preparation

Cut each bean-curd cake into 8 pieces. Deep fry for 3 minutes, and drain. Soak the noodles in water for 5 minutes, and drain. Soak the mushrooms in 1 cup warm water for 1/2 hour.

Reserve the water. Remove the stems and cut each mushroom into quarters. Soak the wood ears in warm water for ½ hour and rinse to clean. Soak the dried bamboo shoots and lily-bud stems for ½ hour and cut into 1-inch sections. Discard water.

Prepare the vegetables by slicing the cabbage into ½-inch slices and breaking the broccoli into 1-inch branches. Cut the celery and green beans into 1 – 1½-inch lengths and the eggplant into ½-inch-thick slices. Crush the garlic, and cut the onion into thin slices.

Cooking
Heat the vegetable oil in a casserole. Add the onion and garlic to stir fry over high heat for 1 minute. Add all the vegetables and butter, and stir fry together for 3 – 4 minutes. Add the salt, soy sauce, bean-curd cheese, sugar, pepper, Vegetable Broth, and mushroom water. Bring to a boil and simmer over low heat for 15 minutes. Add the bean curd and transparent noodles. Turn them in the soup and vegetables. Allow the contents to heat together for 7 – 8 minutes more. Pour in the sherry and sprinkle with sesame oil. Serve in the casserole itself or in a large tureen. Serves 6 – 10.

For nonvegetarians, toss in ½ – ¾ pound red-cooked pork or beef, together with a few tablespoons of gravy, to cook with the vegetables during their stewing. The resulting stew of meat and vegetables is quite irresistible. Not infrequently a whole knuckle end of pork is red-cooked for 1½ – 2 hours and then added to a pot of Lo-Han Dish of Mixed Vegetables and simmered for 15 – 20 minutes before serving.

HOT ASSEMBLY OF SHREDDED BAMBOO SHOOTS AND BEAN CURD WITH STRIPS OF CUCUMBER AND CHINESE MUSHROOMS

1 8–10-oz can bamboo shoots
3 oz dried bamboo shoots
1 cake bean curd
4-inch piece medium cucumber
3 oz Chinese dried mushrooms
1 clove garlic
1 slice ginger root
3 stalks spring onion
oil for deep frying
2 Tb vegetable oil
1/2 tsp salt
1 1/2 Tb light soy sauce
1/2 Tb bean-curd cheese
1/2 cup bean broth (made from 1 lb beans cooked in pressure cooker for 30–35 minutes with 5 cups water)
2 Tb butter
2 Tb white wine or sherry
2 tsp sesame oil

Preparation
Shred the bamboo shoots into strips 1 1/2–2 inches long and 1/4 inch thick. Soak the dried bamboo shoots for 1/2 hour and shred in the same way. Cut the bean curd and unskinned cucumber to same size. Soak the dried mushrooms for 1/2 hour, remove the stems, and cut into similar strips. Crush the garlic, shred the ginger, and cut the spring onions into 1 1/2-inch pieces.

Cooking
Deep fry the bean-curd strips and dried bamboo shoots for 2–3 minutes and drain. Heat the vegetable oil in a saucepan or a frying pan with a cover. Add the ginger, garlic, and half the spring onions. Stir fry for 1/2 minute, add the 2 kinds of bamboo shoots, and continue to stir fry for 3 minutes. Add the

salt, soy sauce, bean-curd cheese, and bean broth. Stir once, cover, and leave to cook for 5–6 minutes. Add the butter, bean curd, mushrooms, the rest of the spring onions, and the cucumber strips. Stir and toss until the 5 kinds of strip are well interwoven. Cook for 3 minutes more. Sprinkle with wine and sesame oil. Toss. Serves 6–8.

HOT ASSEMBLY OF CHESTNUTS, SLICED LOTUS ROOT, GINGKO NUTS, PEANUTS, CHINESE MUSHROOMS, AND BEAN CURD

¼ lb dried lotus root	3 Tb vegetable oil
3 oz Chinese dried mushrooms	2 Tb butter
	3 oz green peas
1 cake bean curd	2 Tb soy sauce
oil for deep frying	½ Tb yeast extract
½ lb fresh chestnuts	½ Tb white bean-curd cheese
¼ lb gingko nuts	½ cup Vegetable Broth
¼ lb peanuts	2 tsp sesame oil

Preparation
Soak the lotus root in water for 1 hour and the mushrooms for ½ hour. Drain. Remove stems from mushrooms. Cut the bean curd into 8 pieces and the lotus root into ¼-inch slices. Deep fry lotus root and bean curd for 3 minutes, and drain. Parboil the chestnuts, gingko nuts, and peanuts, for 15 minutes, and drain. Preheat oven to 325 degrees.

Cooking
Heat 3 tablespoons vegetable oil in a casserole. Add all the nuts and stir fry together for 3 minutes. Add the lotus root, mushrooms, bean-curd pieces, butter, and all the other ingredients except the sesame oil. Turn them around until well mixed. Place the casserole in a preheated oven to cook at 325 degrees for 35 minutes. Sprinkle with sesame oil. Serves 6–8.

CLEAR SIMMERING

Clear simmering requires a much longer cooking period than does hot assembly. In order to maintain the clarity of the soup, which should be like a clear consommé, the dish is usually cooked at a low temperature — 275 – 300 degrees in the oven. Because of this static cooking, every piece of vegetable retains its clear-cut native state and color. To prepare a first-class clear-simmered dish, the broth in which the vegetables are cooked must be specially prepared. Various roots and stems of vegetables that will not produce any cloudiness in the liquid are simmered in water for 1½ – 2 hours, then the broth is strained twice through triple layers of cheesecloth.

The preparation and cutting (or even carving) of the vegetables themselves is done with great care. Then they are parboiled for a couple of minutes before being placed in the broth for the final cooking. The dish derives its ultimate flavor from three sources: the broth; the first group of vegetables, which are simmered in the broth for a long time; and the final group of vegetables, which are simmered in the broth for only a short time. These last provide the freshening effect. The majority of clear-simmered dishes are semisoup dishes, always welcomed by rice eaters. The clear broth required for this purpose can generally be prepared as follows:

CLEAR-SIMMER BROTH

½ lb cabbage stems	¼ lb green beans
½ lb broccoli stems	¼ lb carrots
¼ lb turnips	6 cups water
¼ lb potatoes	1½ tsp salt
¼ lb dried beans	1 Tb light soy sauce

Preparation and Cooking
Clean the vegetables thoroughly, cut into pieces approximately 1½ inches square. Place in a casserole, and add the water and seasonings. Cover and simmer in the oven for 3

hours: 1 hour at 300 degrees, 2 hours at 275 degrees. Strain twice through triple layers of cheesecloth.

Almost any fresh or dried vegetable can be cooked in this broth. But for the best results, usually only one vegetable is used as the main ingredient, and smaller amounts of other fresh or dried vegetables are used as supplementary ingredients.

CLEAR-SIMMERED CHINESE CABBAGE, GREEN CABBAGE, CELERY, OR BROCCOLI

½ lb stem and root of green cabbage	2 cups Clear-Simmer Broth
	½ Tb butter
2 oz Chinese dried mushrooms	1 tsp salt
	1 Tb light soy sauce
1½ lb Chinese cabbage	pepper to taste

Preparation

Clean the stem and root of the green cabbage very thoroughly. Cut into 1½-inch pieces. Parboil for 5–6 minutes, and drain. Soak the mushrooms for ½ hour, remove the stems, and cut into quarters. Slice the Chinese cabbage into 1–1½-inch slices. Preheat the oven to 300 degrees.

Cooking

Place the stem and root of the green cabbage at the bottom of a casserole. Pour in the broth. Bring to a boil and simmer gently in the oven at 300 degrees for ½ hour. Add all the other ingredients, and simmer for ½ hour at the same temperature. Turn the cabbage. Reduce oven temperature to 275 degrees and continue to simmer for a further ¼ hour. Adjust for seasoning if necessary and serve in the casserole. Serves 4–6.

Celery or broccoli may be treated in the same way. The tougher stems and stalks should be parboiled, as for the green cabbage. The great appeal of this dish lies in the sweetness and clarity of flavor of the principal vegetable.

CLEAR-SIMMERED ZUCCHINI, BRUSSELS SPROUTS, OR GREEN BEANS

2 lb large zucchini
1/4 lb cucumber
1 oz Chinese dried mushrooms and/or 1 oz dried bamboo
    shoots
3 cups Clear-Simmer Broth
1/2 Tb butter
1 tsp salt
1 Tb light soy sauce
pepper to taste

Preparation

Clean and scrape the skin of the zucchini, removing tough parts. Cut into 2–3-inch pieces. Cut the unpeeled cucumber into 1-inch sections and then cut vertically into slices 1/6 inch thick, each piece including skin. Soak the mushrooms and/or dried bamboo shoots in warm water for 1/2 hour. Remove the stems from mushrooms. Cut them into quarters and the bamboo shoots into strips. Preheat oven to 300 degrees.

Cooking

Place the bamboo shoots and mushrooms at the bottom of a casserole, pour in the Clear-Simmer Broth, and add the zucchini and butter. Sprinkle with seasonings and flavorers. Place the casserole in the oven to simmer at 300 degrees for 1/2 hour. Add the cucumber and continue to simmer for another 1/2 hour at 275 degrees. Serve in the casserole. Serves 4–6.

If brussels sprouts or green beans are used, they should be parboiled for 3–4 minutes and drained before being placed in the pot.

CLEAR-SIMMERED ASPARAGUS

1 ½ lb asparagus
1 oz Chinese dried mushrooms and/or 1 oz dried bamboo
  shoots
2 cups Clear-Simmer Broth
½ Tb butter
1 tsp salt
1 Tb light soy sauce
pepper to taste

Preparation
Scrape the lower half of the asparagus until quite clean. Cut
each piece of asparagus into two sections (the tip section and
the harder root-stem section). Parboil the root sections for 5 –
6 minutes and drain. Soak the mushrooms and dried bamboo
shoots in warm water for ½ hour. Remove the stems from
mushrooms. Cut each into quarters and the bamboo shoots
into strips. Preheat oven to 300 degrees.

Cooking
Place the tougher ends of the asparagus, the bamboo shoots,
and the mushrooms at the bottom of the casserole. Add the
Clear-Simmer Broth. Simmer in the oven at 300 degrees for
½ hour. Add the asparagus tips and butter, and all the seasonings and flavorers, and simmer for ½ hour longer at 275
degrees. Serves 4 – 6.

   With the Chinese propensity for cross cooking, we naturally find ourselves cooking mixed pots of vegetables, although
as we have already mentioned, clear simmering is generally
used to bring out the flavor of the one main vegetable. As we
have also noted, when several vegetables are cooked together,
cellophane noodles and bean-curd cakes are often cooked
with them. These two binding elements can be used singly or
together. Because they are neutral in flavor, they have the
great advantage of absorbing and retaining the flavors of the
other ingredients and provide a meatlike body.

CLEAR-SIMMERED MIXED VEGETABLES

½ lb cabbage   4 oz cellophane noodles
¼ lb brussels sprouts   3 cups Clear-Simmer Broth
¼ lb zucchini   1 tsp salt
¼ lb broccoli   1½ Tb light soy sauce
¼ lb carrots   pepper to taste
3 oz romaine lettuce   1 Tb chopped chives
2 oz watercress

Preparation
Clean and scrape the vegetables thoroughly, discarding all the unappealing leaves and roots. Cut the cabbage into 1-inch slices, the brussels sprouts into halves or quarters, the broccoli into individual branches, and the carrots slantwise into 1-inch lengths. Chop the lettuce at 1½-inch intervals and the watercress into 1-inch segments. Scrape the skin of the zucchini and cut into 1½-inch pieces. Parboil the cabbage, brussels sprouts, broccoli, and carrots for 3 minutes, and drain. Soak the noodles in warm water for 10 minutes and drain. Preheat oven to 275 degrees.

Cooking
Place the cabbage, brussels sprouts, broccoli, and carrots at the bottom of a casserole. Add the Clear-Simmer Broth, salt, soy sauce, and pepper. Bring to a gentle boil, and place in the oven at 275 degrees for ½ hour. Add the watercress, lettuce, and chives, and cellophane noodles. Simmer for another 20 minutes, and serve in the casserole.

For nonvegetarians, add chicken broth to the Clear-Simmer Broth in equal amounts. In addition, parboil 1 heaping tablespoon dried shrimp and add to simmer with the vegetables from the beginning.

CLEAR-SIMMERED MIXED VEGETABLES WITH VEGETABLE ROOTS

Westerners usually dismiss vegetable roots as coarse, unappealing fare, but the Chinese often regard them as delicacies, if they are prepared with care. They are especially appetizing when served from the kitchens of vegetarian Buddhist monasteries.

Repeat the previous recipe. Add ³⁄₄ pound specially selected large stems or roots of cabbage or broccoli. Clean thoroughly, and cut or carve carefully into oblong pieces approximately 1 inch by ¹⁄₂ inch by ¹⁄₄ inch. Discard any part that is unappealing or imperfect. Parboil for 5 minutes, and drain. Simmer very gently in Clear-Simmer Broth for ¹⁄₂ hour in the oven at 300 degrees, and add them to the other vegetables and their broth. Simmer for 1 hour at 275 degrees. When the dish arrives at the table, the resultant carved pieces of vegetables are picked out with chopsticks and consumed with relish by connoisseurs.

CLEAR-SIMMERED VEGETABLES WITH DRIED AND PICKLED VEGETABLES

The addition of dried and pickled vegetables, which naturally have a much more concentrated flavor than fresh vegetables, will enrich many dishes. Small quantities (1–3 ounces) of these tangy vegetables are added during the simmering. In order to prevent them from overcoloring the broth in the dish, they are generally soaked first, then drained and parboiled for 1–2 minutes before being added to the main mixed stock. The most commonly used dried vegetables are, of course, mushrooms and lily-bud stems; the latter have a distinctive marshy taste with which the Chinese are familiar, but since this may not appeal to the Westerner, they can be omitted. Before serving, 1–2 tablespoons coarsely minced pickles are often scattered over the cooked dish. Wood ears are a variety of fungus used frequently in Chinese cooking; they have little flavor of their own, but are added for their crunchy texture and for the visual contrast their color (usually black) provides.

SAUCES FOR VEGETABLES

As a rule, we Chinese do not go in for made-up sauces, preferring to wait for the sauces to come out of the food as it is cooked. To this, we add a few basic flavorers and seasonings: Vegetable Broth, soy sauce, hoisin sauce, sugar, vinegar, and wine. For nonvegetarian dishes, the basic liquid flavorers are usually concentrated chicken broth (which can be produced by adding chicken-stock cubes to ordinary chicken broth), shrimp sauce, oyster sauce, or red-cooked meat gravy. The addition of these meaty ingredients, or meat essence, turns Chinese vegetable dishes almost into meat dishes; this is the reason for their popularity with lovers of savory food throughout the world. However, Chinese vegetable cooking does use a few very popular made-up sauces, which can easily be added to most vegetable dishes, especially those which are stir fried or stir fried and braised.

HOT BLACK-BEAN AND TOMATO SAUCE (RATATOUILLE CHINOISE)

This sauce, here adapted for Western use, originates from the western Chinese province of Szechuan.

½ Tb salted black beans	4 Tb vegetable oil
1 medium-size onion	½ Tb soybean paste
1 red chili pepper	¾ cup Vegetable Broth
2 cloves garlic	1 Tb soy sauce
2 slices ginger root	½ Tb hoisin sauce
4 medium-size tomatoes	¼ cup red wine
2 medium zucchini	2 tsp sugar
4 small eggplants	1 Tb sesame oil

Preparation
Soak the black beans in water for ½ hour and drain. Chop the onion and pepper into very small pieces, removing seeds. Crush the garlic and ginger. Skin the tomatoes and cut into quarters. Dice the zucchini and eggplants into ½-inch cubes.

Cooking
Heat the vegetable oil in a heavy pan. When hot, add the black beans, pepper, onion, garlic, and ginger. Stir fry for 2 minutes over medium heat. Add the tomatoes, eggplants, zucchini, and soybean paste, and continue to stir fry gently for 5 minutes. Add the Vegetable Broth, soy sauce, and hoisin sauce. Stir and leave to simmer for 20 minutes, placing an asbestos pad under the pan. Add the wine and sugar. Stir and continue to simmer for about 20 minutes, or until the liquid begins to thicken. Add sesame oil. Stir a few more times, and the Ratatouille Chinoise is ready. This quantity will flavor 5–6 portions.

A few tablespoons of this "ratatouille" make a welcome addition to the majority of stir-fried dishes, vegetarian or semivegetarian, or it can be added to boiled rice at the table. The following are some of the stir-fried or stir-braised dishes to which a few tablespoonfuls of Hot Black-Bean and Tomato Sauce (Ratatouille Chinoise) can be added:

PLAIN STIR-FRIED SPINACH

PLAIN STIR-FRIED BEAN SPROUTS

PLAIN STIR-FRIED YOUNG LEEKS

PLAIN STIR-FRIED CHINESE
   CABBAGE

PLAIN STIR-FRIED CELERY

STIR-BRAISED BROCCOLI OR
   CAULIFLOWER

STIR-BRAISED BRUSSELS SPROUTS

SWEET-AND-SOUR SAUCE

This famous Chinese sauce can be added to many meat as well as vegetable dishes.

>   3 Tb tomato purée
>   2 Tb soy sauce
>   2½ Tb sugar
>   3 Tb vinegar
>   2 – 3 Tb fruit juice (orange, pineapple, apple, etc.)
>   ¾ Tb cornstarch (blended in 4 Tb water)
>   2 Tb sherry
>   1 Tb mixed pickles
>   1 Tb vegetable oil
>   4 Tb water

Preparation and Cooking

Mix the first seven ingredients in a bowl and stir until they are well blended. Stir fry the pickles in oil for ½ minute. Pour in the water. When it starts to boil vigorously, pour in the blended sauce mixture. Stir until the mixture thickens and is translucent.

Food that has been stir fried can be cooked for a short time in this sauce and then served, or the sauce can be poured over foods after they have been put in their serving dishes. It is necessary to use enough of this sauce to cover all the foods on the serving dish (not just a couple of tablespoons). This quantity will flavor 4 – 6 portions.

The following are a few of the many dishes to which it can be added:

PLAIN STIR-FRIED BEAN SPROUTS

PLAIN STIR-FRIED CELERY

PLAIN STIR-FRIED TOMATOES

PLAIN STIR-FRIED CHINESE CABBAGE

PLAIN STIR-FRIED OR STIR-BRAISED BROCCOLI OR CAULIFLOWER

PLAIN STIR-FRIED OR STIR-BRAISED EGGPLANT OR ZUCCHINI

MUSHROOM SAUCE

6 large Chinese dried mushrooms
¾ lb mushrooms
2 Tb butter
1½ Tb vegetable oil
1 cup Vegetable Broth
1 Tb soy sauce
½ Tb hoisin sauce
½ Tb cornstarch (blended in 4 Tb water)
1½ tsp sesame oil
1 Tb sherry

Preparation
Soak dried mushrooms in ¾ cup hot water for ½ hour. Remove stems and cut into thin strips. Retain mushroom water. Clean fresh mushrooms and cut into thin slices.

Cooking
Heat the butter in a saucepan. When hot, add the sliced fresh mushrooms, and sauté and stir fry gently for 5–6 minutes. Sauté the strips of dried mushroom in vegetable oil for 5–6 minutes. Combine the mushrooms in one pan, and stir them together for 1 minute. Pour in the Vegetable Broth, add mushroom water, soy sauce, and hoisin sauce. Allow the contents to simmer gently for 15 minutes over low heat, stirring occasionally. Add the cornstarch mixture, sesame oil, and sherry. Stir until the mixture thickens. The sauce is usually poured directly over rice or fried rice. It is a very useful addition when few savory dishes are available. This quantity will flavor 5–6 portions.

FU-YUNG SAUCE

The Chinese Fu-Yung Sauce is a white sauce made with egg white (and for nonvegetarians, usually with minced chicken).

Vegetarians can make it by combining seasoned beaten egg white with a *roux* made from flour, butter, and milk.

    4 egg whites
    3 Tb butter
    2 Tb plain flour
    ½ cup cream
    salt and pepper to taste

Preparation and Cooking
Beat the egg whites with a rotary beater for 15–20 seconds or until they become slightly stiff. Make a *roux* by stirring flour into hot butter in a saucepan and gradually adding cream. Finally stir in the egg white to blend with the *roux*, and season with salt and pepper. (Extra cream is optional, but 2–3 tablespoons may be added here.) Fu-Yung Sauce can be added to most light-colored vegetable dishes in which not too much soy sauce or soybean paste has been used. Its whiteness makes it suitable for green vegetables, such as broccoli, zucchini, cucumber, brussels sprouts, peas, and leeks, particularly when the vegetables have not been cooked in dark-colored sauces; it gives the greenness of the vegetable a glistening and jadelike appearance. This quantity will flavor 4–5 portions.

WILLOW SAUCE

This is a sharp, vinegary sauce usually used by nonvegetarians on fish. For vegetarians who like a pungent sauce, it can be served with other dishes to compensate for any lack of savoriness.

1 medium-size green pepper	3 Tb sugar
2 red chili peppers	2 Tb soy sauce
3 oz bamboo shoots	1 Tb cornstarch
3 oz carrots	1 Tb sherry
2 tomatoes	4 Tb vinegar
1 cup water	½ cup mixed pickles

Preparation
Shred the green pepper, chili peppers, bamboo shoots, and carrots into matchsticks. Skin and cut the tomatoes into quarters, then quarter again.

Cooking
Bring ½ cup water to boil in a saucepan. Add the sugar and soy sauce. Blend the cornstarch, sherry, and vinegar in the remaining ½ cup water. When well blended, pour into the pan. Stir until the liquid thickens. Add the shredded peppers, bamboo shoots, carrots, tomatoes, and pickles. Allow them to simmer gently in the pan for 4–5 minutes. Stir a couple of times and serve in a bowl or sauce boat. The sauce is hot and has a strong tang. It can be added to anything that has a milder taste, such as omelets, bean sprouts, salads, and fish. This quantity will flavor 4–6 portions.

HOT PEANUT-BUTTER SAUCE

In the Fukien Province of China, this sauce is usually made with sesame paste. If it cannot be obtained, peanut butter blended with sesame oil can be used instead.

    3 Tb peanut butter
    2 Tb sesame oil
    2 Tb soy sauce
    2 Tb sherry
    2 Tb sugar
    3 Tb Vegetable Broth
    1 Tb hoisin sauce
    2 Tb tomato purée
    1 tsp chili sauce or ½ tsp Chinese chili oil

Preparation and Cooking
Heat the ingredients together gently for 3 minutes over low heat, stirring continuously. This is a southern sauce, often poured over cooked bean curd, well-cooked hard vegetables, or noodles and other starches. This quantity will flavor 5–6 portions.

SOUPS

THE PRINCIPAL FUNCTIONS of Chinese soups are to provide a savory liquid to swallow when eating quantities of rice and other foods and to give a balance to the variety of dishes on the table. They are meant to be taken throughout the meal and not just as a first course. Therefore, there can be more than one soup served at a meal, placed on the table along with all the other dishes. During a Chinese banquet, the soups often mark the beginnings and ends of different series of dishes.

For full flavor, a Chinese soup is usually made in four stages: (1) preparation of the basic broth; (2) addition of dried, salted, or pickled ingredients to give added flavor or piquancy; (3) cooking of the principal ingredients in the broth, either long, slow cooking or instant; (4) addition of freshening — aromatic or quickly cooked — ingredients toward the last stage of the cooking.

Naturally not all soups involve all four stages. Because a great variety of materials can be used and cross blended in the different stages, the number of soups that can be produced, as with most varieties of Chinese dishes, is again only a matter of permutation.

First of all, let us start with the preparation of the basic broth. In nonvegetarian cooking, it is produced by simmering together chicken, pork, and bones for a long period of time; if a freshener is required, some minced chicken meat is usually added in the final few minutes of cooking before the broth is strained. This results in an extremely tasty and flavorful broth, which can be combined with a vast variety of ingredients to make a first-class soup in a very brief time.

In order to produce a tasty and flavorful vegetarian soup, after the basic broth has been made, greater care has to be exercised in the selection of the principal ingredients and greater attention must also be paid to the selection of dried, pickled, and salted materials for flavoring, and as well as to the fresheners added during the last stages of the cooking. In the modern kitchen, some concessions should be made to Western products, such as yeast extract (or Marmite), which will help to make soups — especially darker ones — savory.

BASIC VEGETABLE BROTH

In China, Basic Vegetable Broth is prepared by the double process of long simmering and short cooking: 2 – 3 vegetables, including dried beans, are long simmered (for 2 – 2½ hours), followed by the short cooking (for 10 – 15 minutes) in the same liquid of 1 – 2 soft vegetables. The liquid is then strained to provide the broth. More elaborately, Basic Vegetable Broth is produced by simmering together 1 unit fresh mushroom stems, ½ unit dried mushrooms, ½ unit peanuts, 1½ units yellow beans (or any other type of dried beans), together with 1 unit vegetables (any 2 – 3 types, such as carrots, turnips, lentils, rutabagas, parsnips, celery, potatoes, onions, cauliflower, or cabbage), in 5 – 6 units water for 2 hours. The broth is then strained and the vegetables are discarded. Finally, the broth is seasoned with soy sauce, salt, pepper, and yeast extract. If ½-pound amounts of vegetables are used, 7 – 8 cups simmering water will be needed to produce 4 – 6 portions of soup.

In dark-colored soups, 1½ tablespoons soy sauce, ½ teaspoon salt, and ½ teaspoon yeast extract (or Marmite) should be added for seasoning. For soups with one predominant flavoring—such as onion, celery, mushroom, or carrot—a bias of ½–1 extra unit of that vegetable can be added together with 1 cup extra water. This basic broth, white or dark, is used for preparing all soups. With a quantity on hand, many Chinese soups can be produced almost instantly. If a nonvegetarian broth is needed, add 1 chicken-stock cube and ½ cup water to the above version of Basic Vegetable Broth.

SIMPLIFIED VEGETABLE BROTH

You will need 1½ pounds vegetables, consisting of any three (or all) of the following vegetables: cabbage, carrots, cauliflower, tomatoes, onions, turnips, leeks, broccoli, brussels sprouts, green beans, and zucchini. Add to them ½ pound mushroom stems. Bring to a boil in 5 cups water, and simmer very gently for 1 hour. Add 1¾ tablespoons soy sauce (if nonvegetarian, add 1 chicken-stock cube), and simmer for another 10 minutes. Strain for use as broth or stock.

QUICK-COOKED SOUPS

As can be anticipated, these soups are prepared from tender vegetables that require a minimum of cooking.

STRIPS OF CUCUMBER SOUP

1 heaping Tb Chinese or other dried mushrooms	1 Tb soy sauce
	½ Tb yeast extract
4 cups Basic Vegetable Broth (dark or white)	salt and pepper to taste
	1 tsp sesame oil
6-inch piece cucumber	1 tsp salad oil

Preparation
Soak the mushrooms in hot water for ½ hour, remove stems, and add to the broth. Cut the cucumber into 3 equal pieces

and scrape out the soft center. Cut the skin and firm outside rim of the cucumber vertically into thin strips ¼ inch wide.

Cooking
Heat the broth in a saucepan, adding soy sauce and yeast extract, and simmer for 1 minute. Add the cucumber strips. Simmer for 3–4 minutes. Adjust for seasoning, sprinkle with sesame oil and salad oil, and serve in a tureen or in individual bowls. Serves 4–5.

SPINACH SOUP

    1 heaping Tb Chinese or other dried mushrooms
    4 cups Basic Vegetable Broth (dark)
    ½ lb best leaf spinach
    1 clove garlic
    1 Tb butter
    ½ Tb vegetable oil
    1 Tb soy sauce
    ½ Tb yeast extract
    salt and pepper to taste
    1 tsp sesame oil

Preparation
Soak the mushrooms in hot water for ½ hour, remove stems, and add to broth. Wash spinach, remove any stalks or unsightly leaves. Crush the garlic.

Cooking
Bring the broth to a boil, and simmer for 1 minute. Heat butter and vegetable oil in a large saucepan. Add garlic and mushrooms, and stir fry for ½ minute. Add the spinach and stir fry over high heat for 1 minute. Pour in the broth, soy sauce, and yeast extract, and simmer for 5 minutes. Adjust for seasonings, sprinkle with sesame oil, and serve in a tureen. Serves 4–5.

GREEN JADE SOUP (CREAM OF SPINACH SOUP)

½ lb chopped or minced fresh or frozen spinach
1 cup canned creamed corn
3 cups Basic Vegetable Broth (white or dark)
½ Tb cornstarch (blended with 2 Tb water)
1½ Tb butter
1 Tb soy sauce
1½ Tb yeast extract
salt and pepper to taste

Preparation
Thaw the spinach if frozen. Mix the creamed corn with the broth and heat together to a simmer. Stir in the cornstarch mixture to thicken it.

Cooking
Heat the butter in a large saucepan. When melted, stir in the spinach. Stir fry for 2 minutes, and pour in the creamed corn and broth mixture. Add the soy sauce and yeast extract. Stir until the spinach is well blended into the liquid. Adjust for seasoning. Simmer for 2 minutes and serve. More butter may be added if a richer soup is desired. Serves 5–6.

All Chinese quick-cooked soups can be prepared in the same manner as Strips of Cucumber Soup and Spinach Soup, with only minor variations: often more shredded dried mushrooms are added to enhance the taste where the mushroom flavor does not conflict with the flavor of the main vegetable in the soup, or one other ingredient—such as egg drop (beaten egg dripped slowly into the soup) or cellophane noodles—is added to provide contrast or variation in color, texture, or substance, or a small quantity of a chopped salted or pickled vegetable is added to give an additional tang or piquancy.

TOMATO SOUP

2 stalks spring onion	1 Tb soy sauce
4 – 5 medium-size tomatoes	1 Tb yeast extract
1 egg	pepper to taste
5 cups Basic Vegetable	1 ½ tsp sesame oil
Broth (dark)	1 Tb dry sherry

Preparation
Finely chop the spring onions. Cut each tomato into six. Beat the egg lightly with a fork.

Cooking
Heat the broth in a saucepan. Lower the heat as soon as it starts to boil. Add the tomatoes, and simmer for 5 minutes. Add the soy sauce and yeast extract. Trail the beaten egg into the soup along the prongs of a fork, in as thin a stream as possible, allowing it to trail over the soup. Pepper the soup liberally; adjust for seasonings. Add the sesame oil and sherry. Sprinkle with spring onions. Serves 5 – 6.

MUSHROOM SOUP

4 medium-size Chinese or other dried mushrooms
8 medium-size mushrooms
5 cups Basic Vegetable Broth (dark)
1 ½ Tb soy sauce
1 Tb yeast extract
2 Tb butter
2 Tb sherry
salt and pepper to taste

Preparation
Soak the dried mushrooms in hot water for ½ hour. Discard the stems and slice into thin strips. Remove the stems of the fresh mushrooms, and slice each into 8 – 10 thin slices.

Cooking
Heat the broth in a saucepan, adding the dried mushrooms. Add the soy sauce and yeast extract. Heat the butter in anoth-

er saucepan, and add the sliced fresh mushrooms. Turn over in the butter a few times, and sauté for 3 minutes. Pour into the broth and dried mushrooms in the first pan, and simmer for 3 minutes. Pour in the sherry and adjust for seasoning. Serves 5 – 6.

WATERCRESS SOUP

Watercress Soup can be quickly prepared in the same manner as Spinach Soup or Strips of Cucumber Soup. The important thing is to wash the watercress thoroughly and remove any muddy roots. You may add 1 – 2 tablespoons chopped pickled Chinese greens (such as red-in-snow) to provide added tang and flavor.

CELERY SOUP

Celery Soup follows the preceding methods, but the celery, sliced diagonally into 2/3-inch segments, should be simmered in the broth for a longer period: 8 – 10 minutes. Generally a few extra tablespoons of Chinese dried mushrooms are used to enhance the flavor, since celery, being a somewhat strongly flavored vegetable, can counterbalance the pronounced taste of the mushrooms in the broth.

LEEK SOUP

Leek Soup can be prepared in the same manner as Celery Soup, and both require about the same cooking time. For 4 – 5 cups Leek Soup, you may add 2 – 3 ounces cellophane noodles. The noodles should be soaked in warm water for about 5 minutes before being added to the broth to simmer with the leeks. As these noodles do not become soft and mushy in cooking, they provide an interesting mixture of taste and texture alongside the dried mushrooms.

LETTUCE SOUP

Lettuce Soup can be prepared in precisely the same manner as Cucumber Soup. Both vegetables require a minimum of cooking time. Indeed soups of either should always be freshly made and drunk immediately after they have been prepared, so that the vegetables do not become limp. In making the soup, choose the crispest lettuce, and cut the leaves into strips 1/4 inch wide. Use the white rather than the dark Basic Vegetable Broth. To enhance the flavor, sprinkle 1/4 – 1/2 tablespoon finely chopped chives or spring onion over the soup before serving, or add a small quantity of watercress (about 1/4 the quantity of lettuce) to simmer together with the lettuce.

EGG-DROP SOUP

Egg-Drop Soup is one of the soups most commonly served in China. It sometimes consists of no more than boiling water with a couple of tablespoons of soy sauce. This is poured into a large soup bowl and lightly beaten egg is trailed into the soup in a very thin stream along the prongs of a fork. The liquid should not be stirred until the egg has coagulated into flowerets. More flavor may be provided by sprinkling 1/4 – 1/2 tablespoon finely chopped chives or spring onion over the soup, along with 1 teaspoon sesame oil. The soup will of course be much tastier if Basic Vegetable Broth (white) is used instead of plain water. An additional tang may be provided by the addition of 1 – 2 teaspoons vinegar.

LONGER-COOKED SOUPS

Because the majority of Chinese soups – apart from instant soups – are clear soups, it is essential to cook them slowly. If cooking is done on top of the stove, an asbestos pad should be placed under the pan. Otherwise, it is a good idea to prepare Chinese soups in a casserole in the oven, where the heating is usually more even and easily controlled.

HOT CABBAGE SOUP

Hot Cabbage Soup may be white or dark, depending on the broth used. For a darker soup, dark soy sauce is added.

    3 Tb Chinese dried mushrooms
    1 red chili pepper
    1 medium cabbage
    6 cups Basic Vegetable Broth
    2 – 2½ Tb soy sauce
    1½ Tb vegetable oil or butter
    salt and pepper to taste

Preparation
Soak the dried mushrooms in hot water for ½ hour. Remove the stems and slice the mushrooms into thin strips. Cut the pepper into 6 – 8 strips, and remove the seeds. Remove the stem from the heart of the cabbage, and cut it into 6 – 8 thin slices. Cut the cabbage leaves into slices ½ inch wide. Preheat oven to 325 degrees.

Cooking
Heat the oil or butter in a casserole. Add the pepper and turn the strips in the oil for ½ minute. Add the cabbage-stem slices, turn them in the oil for 1 minute, and sauté gently for 3 minutes. Add the cabbage leaves, and pour in the broth. Bring to a boil and place the casserole to simmer gently in the oven for ½ hour at 325 degrees. Add the mushroom strips. Adjust for seasonings (add dark soy sauce for a dark soup; salt, light soy sauce, and pepper for a white one), and simmer again for a further 10 – 15 minutes at the same temperature. Serve in a large bowl or tureen or in individual bowls. Serves 6 – 8.

HEART OF CABBAGE SOUP

1½ lb cabbage

2 heaping Tb Chinese or other dried mushrooms

2 Tb butter

5 cups Basic Vegetable Broth

1 Tb soy sauce

1 Tb yeast extract

2 Tb dry sherry

salt and pepper to taste

Preparation

Remove the outer leaves of the cabbage and reserve for use in another dish. Cut the heart vertically into quarters. Soak the mushrooms in hot water for ½ hour, and remove the stems. Preheat the oven to 325 degrees.

Cooking

Heat the butter in a casserole. When it has melted, turn the mushrooms and heart of cabbage in it for 2 minutes. Pour in the broth and add the soy sauce and yeast extract. Bring to a boil, and place the casserole in a preheated oven at 325 degrees for 45 minutes. Add sherry and salt and pepper.

Serving

The soup can be served either in the casserole or in individual bowls. One of the attractions of this soup is that the heart of cabbage becomes extremely tender, yet still retains its neat original shape. Serves 5–6.

TURNIP SOUP

Turnips are used in soups far more frequently in China than in the West. Nonvegetarians usually cook them with beef broth or broth from some other strong-tasting meat, such as mutton, while vegetarians often use a slightly stronger Basic Vegetable Broth (made by adding 3–4 tablespoons dried mushrooms instead of fresh mushrooms, and 2 slices ginger root). Turnip Soup is cooked in exactly the same way as the Heart of Cabbage Soup in the previous recipe, except that it is simmered for 1¼–1½ hours in a casserole in the oven at 325 degrees. To serve 5–6, use ¾–1 pound turnips, sliced diagonally into ½-inch pieces, to 5 cups strengthened broth.

ASPARAGUS AND BAMBOO-SHOOT SOUP

1 lb fresh asparagus
4 oz canned bamboo shoots
3 oz dried bamboo shoots
1½ Tb vegetable oil
6 cups Basic Vegetable Broth

1 Tb soy sauce
1 Tb yeast extract
2 Tb sherry
1 tsp sesame oil
salt and pepper

Preparation
Remove the tough parts at the base of the asparagus. Slice the remainder diagonally into 1½-inch segments. Cut the canned bamboo shoots into pieces of approximately the same size. Soak the dried bamboo shoots in hot water for ½ hour. Slice into thin strips. Preheat oven to 325 degrees.

Cooking
Heat the vegetable oil in a casserole. Add the dried bamboo shoots and stir fry for two minutes. Pour in the broth, add the asparagus, canned bamboo shoots, soy sauce, and yeast extract. Bring to a boil, and place the casserole in a preheated oven for 1 hour at 325 degrees. Remove the casserole from the oven. Add the sherry and sesame oil, and salt and pepper to taste. Serves 6–8.

BRUSSELS-SPROUT SOUP

¾ lb brussels sprouts
3 oz dried bamboo shoots
1 oz hot-pickled Szechuan
   cabbage
2 Tb butter

5 cups Basic Vegetable Broth
1½ Tb soy sauce
½ Tb yeast extract
salt and pepper

Preparation
Clean the brussels sprouts and remove any unsightly outer leaves. Cut each sprout into quarters. Soak the dried bamboo

shoots in hot water for ½ hour. Slice into 1-inch-thin strips. Slice the Szechuan cabbage into thin pieces. Preheat oven to 300 degrees.

Cooking
Heat the butter in a casserole. When melted, add the Szechuan cabbage and dried bamboo shoots, and stir fry for 2 minutes. Add the broth and sprouts, soy sauce, and yeast extract. Bring to a boil, and place the casserole in a preheated oven at 300 degrees for 1 hour. Adjust for seasonings. Serves 4 – 6.

BROCCOLI SOUP

Broccoli Soup can be prepared in precisely the same manner as the Brussels-Sprout Soup in the previous recipe. Cut the broccoli into small individual branches. A small quantity of cellophane noodles may be added to give variety to the texture.

MIXED VEGETABLE SOUP

2 medium-size onions	2 oz cellophane noodles
3 oz water chestnuts	2 Tb butter
3 oz carrots	5 cups Basic Vegetable Broth
3 oz green beans	(white)
3 oz cabbage	1 Tb yeast extract
3 oz celery	salt and pepper
3 oz dried bamboo shoots	1½ Tb cornstarch (blended
2 heaping Tb Chinese or	in 6 Tb milk)
other dried mushrooms	(optional)

Preparation
Cut all the vegetables diagonally into ½-inch-thick slices or segments. Soak the dried bamboo shoots and dried mushrooms in hot water for ½ hour. Remove mushroom stems. Slice thinly. Preheat oven to 300 degrees.

Cooking
Heat the butter in a casserole. Add the dried bamboo shoots and stir fry for 2 minutes. Add all the other vegetables and stir fry for 3 – 4 minutes. Pour in the broth, add the noodles, yeast extract, and salt and pepper to taste. Bring to the boil, and place casserole in a preheated oven at 300 degrees for 1 hour. Adjust for seasoning. Thicken with a milk and corn-starch mixture, if desired. Serves 5 – 6.

CHINESE ONION SOUP

8 medium-size onions	1 Tb yeast extract
2 heaping Tb Chinese dried mushrooms	salt and pepper
	1 Tb cornstarch (blended in 4 Tb water)
2 Tb butter	
5 cups Basic Vegetable Broth	1 Tb vegetable oil
2 Tb soy sauce	3 Tb chopped watercress

Preparation
Slice 6 onions into thin slices, and place in one pile. Slice the other 2 onions and place in a separate pile. Soak the mushrooms in hot water for ½ hour. Slice into thin slices, discarding the stems. Preheat oven to 325 degrees.

Cooking
Heat the butter in a casserole. Stir fry the larger pile of onion in the butter for 3 minutes. Pour in the broth, and add the mushrooms, soy sauce, and yeast extract. Adjust seasonings. When the contents start to boil, place the casserole in a pre-heated oven at 325 degrees for 1 hour and 20 minutes. Stir the contents every 20 minutes. After 1 hour, add the blended cornstarch to thicken contents.

Serving
While the casserole is cooking in the oven, heat the oil in a small frying pan, and stir fry the smaller pile of onion gently for 4 – 5 minutes, until slightly brown. When the contents of the casserole are about ready, place the frying pan with the onions under the broiler and toast them until quite crisp. Mix

these onions with chopped watercress and use to garnish the soup, which may be served in the casserole, a large tureen, or individual bowls. Serves 4 – 6.

THICK SOUPS

Although most Chinese soups are clear, there are a number of thick soups. They are usually prepared with bean curd, peas, long-cooked rice, and egg whites (Fu-Yung). Some of them are "sweet" soups, taken as refreshments in the afternoon (and indeed they are very stimulating and sustaining late in the day, as I have lately experienced after strenuous tennis!). They may also serve as a kind of punctuation between a long series of savory dishes during party dinners.

SWEET RICE (CONGEE)

Sweet Rice is the Chinese version of rice pudding, but it is prepared without using milk or cream.

   ½ – ¾ cup glutinous rice
   ¼ cup red beans
   6 cups water
   1 cup mixed glacé fruits and nuts, including dates, lotus
      seeds (optional), almonds, peanuts, sugared ginger, etc.
   4 – 5 Tb sugar
   1 Tb honey

Cooking
Wash the rice and place in a heavy pan with the red beans. Add the water and bring to a boil. Turn heat as low as possi-

ble and place an asbestos pad under the pan. Stir every 15 minutes. After 45 minutes, add the nuts and fruits. Continue to simmer gently and stir every 20 minutes or so for an hour longer. Stir in the sugar and honey and blend well.

In the Western kitchen, a simplified version of this recipe can be prepared by heating a cupful of dried fruits and nuts in 1 cup milk for 10–15 minutes with 2 tablespoons sugar. Then stir in 1 can rice pudding. But we Chinese feel that the Sweet Rice is more refreshing without milk or cream.

SWEET PEANUT SOUP

    4 cups water
    1 tsp baking soda
    2 cups unroasted peanuts
    1 Tb cornstarch (blended in 4 Tb water)
    4–5 Tb brown sugar
    1 Tb honey

Cooking
Heat the water in a heavy pan. Stir in the baking soda. When it boils, add the peanuts. Turn heat as low as possible and place an asbestos pad under the pan. Stir every 15 minutes and continue to heat for 1½ hours. Add cornstarch and water mixture to thicken. Stir in the sugar and honey and blend well.

SWEET PEA SOUP

Repeat the preceding recipe using 2 cups dried split peas instead of peanuts. The peas will first have to be soaked overnight and then simmered in 3⅓ cups water for 1½–2 hours. Before adding cornstarch, sugar, and honey, strain the soup through a fine sieve, then reheat for 1 minute. This is a refreshing soup that provides a sustaining snack at any time of the day.

GREEN AND WHITE SOUP

White portion
4 egg whites
½ cup milk
¼ cup cream
1 cup Basic Vegetable Broth (white)
1 Tb cornstarch (blended in 3 Tb water)
1 tsp salt

Green portion
1½ Tb butter
½ lb chopped or minced spinach
2 cups Basic Vegetable Broth (dark)
½ Tb yeast extract
½ tsp salt
1½ tsp sugar
1½ Tb cornstarch (blended in 6 Tb water)

Preparation
Beat the egg whites with a rotary beater for 15 seconds. Add all the other ingredients for the white portion and blend well.

Cooking
Heat the butter in a saucepan. When it has melted, pour in the spinach and turn it in the butter for 1 minute. Pour in the 2 cups broth. When hot, add all the other ingredients for the green portion. Stir until the liquid begins to boil and thicken. Allow to simmer gently for 2–3 minutes.

See that all the ingredients for the white portion are well blended, stir up again if necessary. Pour into a saucepan. Heat until the liquid begins to boil and thicken.

Serving
Pour the green soup into a large soup bowl or tureen, and pour the white soup into the center of the green soup, being careful not to mix the two. Ladle out and serve in individual bowls.

GREEN-PEA SOUP

²/₃ lb green peas
2 Tb butter
3 cups Basic Vegetable Broth (white)
¹/₂ Tb yeast extract
1 tsp salt
1¹/₂ Tb cornstarch (blended in 6 Tb water)
1 cup milk

Preparation
Add the peas to 2 cups boiling water. Heat for 20 minutes. Drain, and purée in an electric blender until smooth and creamy.

Cooking
Heat the butter in a saucepan. Add the peas. Turn and blend with the butter. Pour in the broth. When hot, add all the other ingredients. Stir until the liquid begins to boil and thicken. Heat gently for another 3 minutes. Serves 4–6.

RED-BEAN CONGEE (SOFT RICE)

This is a sweet soup, with a puddinglike consistency, usually eaten on its own as a snack. It is excellent on a wintry day.

¹/₂ cup Patna or other long-grained rice
5 cups water
¹/₂ lb red beans
4 cups water
4–6 Tb sugar to taste

Preparation and Cooking
Wash the rice and place in a heavy pan with 5 cups water. Place an asbestos pad under the pan, bring to the boil, simmering very gently for 1¹/₂ hours.

Place the red beans in another saucepan with 4 cups water. Bring to the boil and heat very gently for 1¹/₂ hours.

Combine the red beans with the rice. Stir and blend well, and continue to heat very gently (with the asbestos pad still under the pan) for another 40–50 minutes, stirring every 10 minutes. Add sugar and serve in individual bowls. Serves 4–6.

BASIC BEAN-CURD SOUP

2 cakes bean curd
4 cups Basic Vegetable Broth
1 tsp salt
1 tsp yeast extract

1 Tb soy sauce
1 tsp yellow bean-curd cheese
1 Tb cornstarch (blended in 3 Tb water)

Preparation
Cut the bean curd into ½–1-inch cubes.

Cooking
Heat the broth in a saucepan. Add the salt, yeast extract, soy sauce, and bean-curd cheese. Mix well and add the cornstarch blended in water. Stir until the soup thickens slightly. Add the bean curd. Heat through for 3–4 minutes. Serves 5–6.

ENRICHED BEAN-CURD SOUP

Enriched Bean-Curd Soup can be produced by simmering a number of additional ingredients in the Basic Bean-Curd Soup before adding the bean curd; for example, mushrooms (4 large dried mushrooms, soaked in hot water for ½ hour and diced into ⅙–¼-inch square pieces), spring onions (2 stalks chopped into ¼-inch segments), lily-bud stems (soaked for 1 hour in hot water and then chopped into ¼-inch segments), ¼ cup green peas. After these additional ingredients have been simmered for ½ hour, add 1 salted duck egg (chopped), 1 tablespoon butter, and stir in ½ cup heavy cream. Finally add the bean curd. When bean curd has heated through (3–4 minutes), the soup will be ready to serve.

HOT-AND-SOUR SOUP

The well-known Hot-and-Sour Soup is an extension of the
Enriched Bean-Curd Soup. It is made by blending 2 tablespoons vinegar, 2 tablespoons soy sauce, ½ teaspoon black
pepper (or to taste) and 1½ tablespoons cornstarch in 6 tablespoons Basic Vegetable Broth. Stir this mixture into the Enriched Bean-Curd Soup, which must be hot. When the soup
is further thickened, beat an egg lightly, and trail it into the
soup very slowly, along the prongs of a fork, in as thin a
stream as possible. After about 10 seconds the egg will have
coagulated and formed into egg drops. Give the soup a stir
and serve.

*For nonvegetarians, a few tablespoons of chopped shrimp or
chicken may be added to the broth before it thickens.*

FU-YUNG SOUP

1 Tb butter	2 tsp light soy sauce
½ cup mashed potato	1 Tb cornstarch (blended
1½ cups milk	in 3 Tb water)
1½ cups Basic Vegetable	½ cup cream
Broth (white)	4 egg whites
8-oz can creamed corn	1 salted duck-egg yolk
1½ tsp salt	

Preparation and Cooking
Heat the butter and mashed potato in a saucepan. Add the
milk slowly. Stir and mix continually until the mixture is
well blended. Pour in the broth and creamed corn. Add the
salt, soy sauce, and cornstarch mixture. Stir until well
blended. Add the cream. Beat the egg whites with a rotary
beater until nearly stiff. Stir the egg whites into the soup.
Heat gently for 2 minutes. Pour into a serving bowl. Garnish
with chopped egg yolk. Serves 4 – 5.

RICE

RICE, in vegetable or vegetarian dishes, is prepared and served in four main ways in China: as Vegetable Rice (when the vegetables are cooked or steamed in the rice), as Topped Rice (when a savory vegetable or vegetarian dish is used as a substantial garnish on top of cooked rice), as Fried Rice (when several chopped vegetable items are stir fried together with cooked rice), and as Soft Rice (also known as congee, which is a watery rice porridge, with vegetables slow simmered in it).

Patna rice is the best to use for all the recipes that follow, but any other long-grained rice will do.

BASIC BOILED RICE

There are many ways to boil rice. In China it is very often steamed, but in the West these are two of the easiest ways to prepare it:

1. Place the rice in a heavy pan. Add 1⅔ its volume of water. Cover. Bring to a boil. Place an asbestos pad under the pan. Simmer gently for 8 minutes. Turn off the heat, but leave the rice to cook in its own heat for another 10 minutes.

It should then be ready. Lift the cover *only* when the cooking is done or when you are ready to serve.

2. Place the rice in a casserole. Add 1²/₃ its volume of water. Bring to a boil, cover the casserole, and place in an oven preheated to 350 degrees. After 10 minutes turn off the heat, and leave the rice to cook in its own heat in the oven for another 10 minutes.

VEGETABLE RICE

So-called Vegetable Rice is prepared in China by cooking the rice with a given vegetable or vegetables in the proportion of 2 units of rice to 1 of vegetable. A small amount of salt and oil or butter is also added when the cooking is started. The aim of the dish is to produce rice that has been impregnated with the flavor of the vegetable. This is not a complete dish in itself; it is usually eaten with 2 or 3 savory vegetable dishes. It is customary for the diners to sprinkle Vegetable Rice with a few drops of soy sauce.

GREEN-PEA AND MUSHROOM VEGETABLE RICE

¼ lb mushrooms
½ lb green peas
2 cups rice
3½ cups water
1 tsp salt
1½–2 Tb butter

Clean and rinse mushrooms twice. Place all the ingredients in a casserole. Bring to the boil, stir contents once, cover, and place the casserole in a preheated 350-degree oven for 15 minutes. Turn off the heat, and leave the rice and vegetables to cook in their own heat for 15 minutes.

CARROT, WATERCRESS, AND CUCUMBER VEGETABLE RICE

Follow the recipe for Green-Pea and Mushroom Vegetable Rice, substituting ½ pound each carrots and cucumber. Scrape and dice the carrots into ¼-inch cubes. Leave the skin on the cucumber and dice also into ¼-inch cubes. Slice ¼ pound watercress at 1-inch intervals. At the start of the cooking, spread the vegetables under the rice before adding the water.

BAMBOO-SHOOT VEGETABLE RICE WITH LILY-BUD STEMS

Use ½ pound fresh or canned bamboo shoots with ¼ pound dried bamboo shoots, ¼ pound green peas, and 2 lily-bud stems. Soak the lily-bud stems for 1 hour, drain, and cut into 2-inch segments. Soak the dried bamboo shoots for the same length of time, and cut into 1½-inch pieces. Otherwise proceed in the same manner as in the previous recipes.

TOPPED RICE

Topped Rice means rice that is served with a portion of one of the stir-fried, red-cooked, white-cooked, or marinaded dishes on top of it. In fact, almost any savory dish that has a flavorful gravy is suitable. You can enhance the flavor by supplementing the dish used for the garnish with a few tablespoons of one of the Sauces for Vegetables (see pages 82–87), such as Hot Black-Bean and Tomato Sauce, Sweet-and-Sour Sauce, Mushroom Sauce, Fu-Yung Sauce, Hot Peanut-Butter Sauce, or even the Willow Sauce (the last should be used with caution since it is very vinegary). Topped Rice is especially suitable for the average Western meal because it is served in individual portions, rather than in the usual Chinese buffet style, where a whole range of dishes — or at least 3 or 4 — have to be prepared to make up a proper meal.

FRIED RICE

In vegetarian cooking, Fried Rice is made by stir frying cooked rice with a quantity of chopped onion and one or two salted or dried vegetables — such as braised bamboo shoots, salted turnips, or red-in-snow — and scrambled eggs. The items to be added to the rice are stir fried for a time before the final assembly. Color contrast and difference in texture can be achieved by the addition of green peas, chopped mushrooms, and sweet corn. The aim in Fried Rice is to produce a colorful dish of rice that is light, tasty, and aromatic. In fact, Fried Rice might be described as a hot "rice salad." What must always be avoided in Fried Rice is a mishmash of unrecognizable components. To prevent this, many of the items, such as peas, mushrooms, and corn, should be stir fried separately — as should the egg, which should be set first — before the ensemble is assembled in the final stir frying. In addition, the cooked rice should be thoroughly cooled in order to keep the grains as separate as possible.

In nonvegetarian cooking, Fried Rice contains — in addition to the rice, onion, and scrambled eggs — chopped ham or bacon, instead of the salted or dried vegetables.

VEGETARIAN FRIED RICE I

½ tsp salt
4 eggs
4 oz braised bamboo shoots
2 – 3 oz salted or braised turnips (optional)
1½ oz red-in-snow (optional)
1 large onion
3 oz fresh mushrooms or 2 oz dried mushrooms
3½ Tb vegetable oil
2 Tb butter
3 oz canned corn
3 oz green peas
6 cups cold cooked rice (dry and in separate grains)
1½ Tb soy sauce
½ Tb sesame oil

Preparation
Add the salt to the eggs and beat with a fork for 10 seconds.
Dice the bamboo shoots, turnips, red-in-snow. Do the same
with the onion, keeping it separate. Rinse the mushrooms in
water if fresh; soak in hot water first for ½ hour if dried and
discard stems. Dice mushrooms.

Cooking
Heat the onion in 2½ tablespoons vegetable oil in a small
frying pan over medium heat. Stir fry for 1 minute. Add the
beaten eggs. When the eggs are about to set, scramble lightly.
In another pan, heat the bamboo shoots, turnips, and red-in-
snow in 1 tablespoon oil for 1 minute. Add the butter, mushrooms, corn, and peas. Stir fry together for 2 minutes.

Heat the rice in a large saucepan over medium heat for 1
minute. Add the egg and onion mixture. Toss and turn to
mix it with the rice. Pour the ingredients from the other pan
into the rice. Add soy sauce and sesame oil. Stir, turn, and
mix them all together, still on medium heat. Lift the rice
slightly each time you stir and turn, so that it will not stick.
Toss and stir for 2 minutes. Serves 6.

VEGETARIAN FRIED RICE II

1 large onion	½ tsp salt
2 stalks spring onion	4½ Tb vegetable oil
3 oz braised bamboo shoots	1 Tb butter
2 oz canned or fresh bamboo shoots	3 oz green peas
	3 oz canned corn
3 oz fresh mushrooms or 2 oz dried mushrooms	2 oz raisins
	6 cups cold boiled rice
2 salted duck eggs	1½ Tb soy sauce
4 fresh eggs	

Preparation

Cut the large onion into thin slices. Slice the spring onions into ½-inch segments, using the green parts. Dice the braised bamboo shoots, the canned or fresh bamboo shoots, and the mushrooms into pea-sized cubes (if the mushrooms are dried, soak in hot water first for ½ hour and discard stems). Chop the salted eggs into the same-size cubes. Beat the fresh eggs and salt for 10 seconds with a fork.

Cooking

In a frying pan, stir fry the sliced large onion in 2½ tablespoons vegetable oil for 1 minute over medium heat. Pour in the beaten eggs. Scramble the eggs lightly just before they have set. Remove from heat and keep hot. Heat 2 tablespoons vegetable oil in another frying pan. Add the bamboo shoots and mushrooms, and stir fry together for 1½ minutes. Add the butter, peas, corn, and raisins. Stir fry together for 2 minutes.

Heat the rice in a large saucepan over medium heat. Pour in the contents of both frying pans. Turn and stir until all the items are well mixed. Lift the mixture each time you turn it and stir the rice to ensure that it is light and separated. Sprinkle the chopped salted eggs, spring onions, and soy sauce over the rice. Turn a few times more. Serves 6.

SOFT RICE (CONGEE)

Plain soft rice, or congee, like porridge, is usually eaten at breakfast time in China, accompanied by such things as salted roast peanuts, pickled vegetables, soy-marinated vegetables, salted preserved eggs, etc. Savory soft rice is usually eaten as a snack. A great variety of savory soft-rice dishes can be devised—especially for nonvegetarians—since there are countless savory foods that can be cooked and simmered in soft rice to make very tasty and appetizing combinations. For vegetarians, the variations are fewer, being limited to the vegetables that will make an interesting combination with soft rice; these are a mixture of nuts with root and leaf vegetables, together with the salted, pickled, and soy-braised vegetables.

BASIC SOFT RICE

½ lb rice
2 – 2½ qts water (quantity depending on thickness of the soft rice required)

Preparation and Cooking
Wash and rinse the rice a couple of times. Put it in a heavy pan and add water. Bring to a boil and lower heat to the minimum, placing an asbestos pad under the pan. Simmer the rice very gently for 1½ – 2 hours, stirring with a wooden spoon every 15 – 20 minutes. By the end of this time, the rice will have become a thickish, extremely bland gruel. It is this blandness that gives it a refreshing quality and makes it ideal to be relished with salty, preserved, and highly savory foods.

SAVORY SOFT RICE I

½ lb rice	1 tsp salt
2 – 2½ qts water	3 Tb red-in-snow
¼ lb carrots	2 Tb soy sauce
½ lb cabbage	1 tsp bean-curd cheese
2 salted duck eggs	2 tsp sesame oil
¼ lb peanuts	

Preparation and Cooking

Prepare the soft rice in the same manner as in the basic recipe. Clean the carrots and cabbage thoroughly. Dice the carrots and eggs into ¼-inch cubes, and cut the cabbage, including most of the stem, into 2-inch pieces. After the rice has been cooking for ½ hour, add the peanuts, salt, and carrots. Add the cabbage ½ hour later. When the soft rice is almost ready, stir in the red-in-snow, duck eggs, soy sauce, bean-curd cheese, and sesame oil. Savory soft rice made in this way can be eaten on its own, but more often it accompanies two or three savory dishes, vegetarian or nonvegetarian.

SAVORY SOFT RICE II

½ lb rice	4 – 6 eggs
2 – 2½ qts water	4 – 6 Tb dark soy sauce
6 oz water chestnuts	8 – 12 Tb Hot Black-Bean and
6 oz watercress	Tomato Sauce
2 Tb light soy sauce	

Preparation

Prepare the soft rice as in the previous recipes. Cut the water chestnuts into thin slices. Clean and slice the watercress at 1½-inch intervals.

Cooking

After the rice has cooked for 30 minutes, add the water chestnuts. Cook for 30 minutes. Add the watercress and light soy sauce. Just before the soft rice is ready to serve, break the eggs into it to poach.

Serving
Divide the soft rice into 4–6 bowls, each with a poached egg.
Over each egg pour 1 tablespoon dark soy sauce and 2 table-
spoons Hot Black-Bean and Tomato Sauce. Serves 4–6.

SAVORY SOFT RICE III

    10 oz bean sprouts
    4 Tb red-in-snow
    6 large Chinese dried mushrooms
    4 salted duck eggs
    ½–¾ lb rice
    2–2½ qts water
    2 Tb light soy sauce
    2 Tb butter
    4 Tb dark soy sauce
    9 Tb Mushroom Sauce

Preparation
Clean the bean sprouts thoroughly and drain. Chop the red-
in-snow into coarse grains. Soak the dried mushrooms in hot
water for ½ hour, slice into matchstick strips, and discard
stems. Cut each salted egg into 10 slices and then quarter
each slice.

Cooking
Prepare the basic soft rice as in the previous recipes. When it
has cooked for 1½ hours, add the salted eggs, bean sprouts,
mushroom strips, and light soy sauce. Add the red-in-snow
and butter 5 minutes before serving. Stir gently until all the
ingredients are well mixed.

Serving
Divide the soft rice into 4–6 bowls. Pour just under 1 tablespoon dark soy sauce and 2 tablespoons Mushroom Sauce
into each bowl and serve. Keep any balance hot for second
helpings. Serves 4–6.

NOODLES, WRAPLINGS, AND DUMPLINGS

DISHES BASED on processed starches — doughs — in a large array of forms, sizes, and textures rank next to rice as the most important staple food of China. They come in three main forms: (1) noodles (*meins*), (2) wraplings (*chiaotze*), and (3) steamed dumplings (*paotze*).

NOODLES

Noodles may be served in soups or sauces, or fried (as in Chow Mein), or they can be tossed (as one does with salads).

TOSSED NOODLES I

2 stalks spring onion	1½ tsp sugar
4 oz bean sprouts	1 Tb Vegetable Broth
1 lb noodles	1 Tb sherry
2 Tb butter	4 oz cucumber
3 Tb vegetable oil	3 oz radish
3 Tb soy sauce	6 Tb Mushroom Sauce
½ Tb soybean paste	small bowl containing ½ cup
½ Tb hoisin sauce	vinegar and 1 Tb sesame oil

Preparation and Cooking
Cut the spring onions into ½-inch segments. Rinse and clean the bean sprouts. Boil the noodles for 7–8 minutes, drain, and keep hot. Add the butter, sprinkle with spring onions, toss, and divide into 3–4 bowls—depending on the number to be served. Heat the vegetable oil in a small frying pan over medium heat. Add the soy sauce, soybean paste, hoisin sauce, sugar, Vegetable Broth, and sherry. Stir for 50 seconds or until the mixture is smooth and getting a rich consistency. Shred the cucumber and radish into matchsticks. Put each, and the bean sprouts, in separate bowls.

Serving
Place 1 bowl noodles in front of each person. Pour into each bowl 1½ tablespoons heated Mushroom Sauce and 1½ tablespoons mixed sauce from the pan. Pour the remainder of the mixed sauce into a bowl. Place the various bowls of bean sprouts, cucumber, radish, and vinegar alongside the bowl of mixed sauce for the diners to help themselves. After taking a helping from each bowl, the diner tosses the raw vegetable strips and sesame oil and vinegar with the sauces and cooked noodles already in his bowl. The interest in this dish lies in the contrast between the raw, crunchy vegetable strips and the softness of the noodles, and also between the blandness of the noodles and the sharpness of the sauces and aromatic vinegar. Naturally the quantity of sauces and ingredients can be varied according to taste. Serves 3–4.

TOSSED NOODLES II

Repeat the previous recipe, using 6–7 tablespoons Hot Black-Bean and Tomato Sauce and 4 tablespoons Hot Peanut-Butter Sauce in place of the Mushroom Sauce and the pan sauce. When the noodles are first tossed with the chopped spring onions and butter, 1 additional tablespoon hot salad oil should be added. For the rest, the noodles are served in the same manner as in the previous recipe, permitting the diner to make his own choice of the quantities of raw vegetable strips and vinegar and sesame oil to be tossed with his or her own bowl of noodles.

CHOW MEIN (FRIED NOODLES)

The difference between dishes of tossed noodles and of fried noodles (Chow Mein) is that in the latter cases, it is not the diner who mixes the ingredients but the cook in the kitchen. With fried noodles, the mixing is done in a hot frying pan with more oil and the addition of one or more crunchy ingredients, such as strips of shredded bamboo shoots, cabbage, bean sprouts, and onions. Just before serving, a quantity of savory ingredients (for vegetarians, usually stir-fried or braised foods) is placed on the noodles; these may be mushrooms, green beans, celery, cabbage, peas, snow peas, spinach, pickles, etc. The savory elements should amount to about $1/4 - 1/3$ the weight of the noodles themselves. Thus Chow Mein or fried noodles is, in fact, a kind of double-decker dish.

CHOW MEIN I

1 lb noodles
1 – 2 cloves garlic
1 medium-size onion
3 oz bamboo shoots
3 – 4 oz cabbage
4 large Chinese dried mushrooms
4 oz fresh mushrooms
3 Tb vegetable oil
3 Tb butter
3 Tb soy sauce
4 Tb Hot Black-Bean and Tomato Sauce
$1/2$ Tb sesame oil
$1/4$ Tb hoisin sauce

1 Tb sherry
pepper to taste
$\frac{1}{2}$ tsp sugar

Preparation

Boil the noodles for 7 – 8 minutes, drain, and rinse under running water to prevent sticking. Crush garlic, and cut the onion into thin slices. Slice the bamboo shoots and cabbage into $\frac{1}{4}$-inch-long strips, and parboil for 3 minutes. Soak the dried mushrooms in hot water for $\frac{1}{2}$ hour, remove the stems, and slice into matchsticks. Wash and slice the fresh mushrooms into strips of the same size. Discard the stems.

Cooking

Heat the vegetable oil and 1 tablespoon butter in a frying pan over medium heat. Add the garlic and onion, and stir fry for 1 minute. Add the cabbage and bamboo shoots, and continue to stir fry for 3 minutes. Add the cooked noodles, sprinkle with 2 tablespoons soy sauce, turn and mix with the bamboo shoots and cabbage over medium heat for 3 – 4 minutes, until the ingredients are cooked through and well mixed. Spread these ingredients on a well-heated serving dish and keep hot in the oven. Heat the Hot Black-Bean and Tomato Sauce with sesame oil in a small pan over low heat.

Heat 2 tablespoons butter in a small pan over medium heat. Add the dried mushrooms and stir fry for 1 minute. Add the fresh mushrooms and stir fry for another minute. Add 1 tablespoon soy sauce, the hoisin sauce, sherry, pepper, and sugar. Stir fry together for 2 minutes.

Serving

Pour the mushrooms in the middle of the hot noodles. Pour the Hot Black-Bean and Tomato Sauce in a circle around the mushrooms. Place in the center of the table for the diners to help themselves. Serves 3 – 4.

CHOW MEIN II

Repeat the previous recipe, using 3 ounces braised bamboo shoots (available in cans) and 6 ounces bean sprouts, instead of bamboo shoots and cabbage, for a crunchy effect. Mushroom Sauce can be used instead of Hot Black-Bean and Tomato Sauce.

Alternatively, 2-3 ounces snow peas or green beans cut into 1-2-inch segments and 2 ounces green peas can be stir fried with the mushrooms for an additional couple of minutes, with a slight increase of flavoring ingredients, and used as a garnish along with the mushrooms. The fresh peas and beans will increase the color appeal of the dish. During the stir frying, a couple of tablespoons Vegetable Broth and ½ teaspoon chili sauce may be added.

For nonvegetarians, the noodles are usually stir fried with 3-4 ounces meat—pork or chicken cut into matchsticks and stir fried with garlic and onion at the outset; and shredded beef, lamb, crabmeat, or shrimp can be added to stir fry with the mushrooms, beans, and peas, and used as a garnish.

Such double-decker combinations provide a reasonably substantial snack. The excellence of a dish of this kind, vegetarian or otherwise, depends on the freshness and savoriness of the garnish used, and the right modulation of the crunchiness and taste of the vegetables with the softness of the noodles. When these combinations are right, the dish becomes a classic. But it can also turn into a mess if everything is put in to stir fry together instead of being cooked separately.

WRAPLINGS (CHIAOTZE)

Wraplings are foods or stuffings wrapped in a thin dough skin shaped like a pouch, about the size of an average egg but somewhat thinner and more elongated. Wraplings are usually steamed or boiled, occasionally fried, or sometimes part steamed and part fried. They are eaten as snacks. In North China, when a dozen or a score of them are consumed at a time, they are treated as a meal. The dough skin should be thin and lightly brushed with oil. When made in this way, wraplings become slightly transparent when cooked. Almost any kind of savory food can be used as stuffing, but those that require longer cooking should be stir fried first before they are wrapped in the dough skin.

WRAPLING SKIN

4½ cups plain flour
1 tsp salt
1 cup boiling water
½ cup vegetable oil

Sift the flour and salt into a bowl. Slowly stir in the boiling water, and blend until the mixture is smooth. Cover the bowl and leave to stand for ½ hour.

Place the dough on a well-oiled board, and knead with hands and fingers that have been rubbed with oil. Knead until the dough has become bouncy and elastic. Shape the dough into a roll about 1 inch in diameter, cut off ¼-inch disks, and form each into a small ball. Flatten these with a rolling pin, making a pancake about 3 – 3½ inches in diameter. Place 1 – 2 teaspoonfuls stuffing just below the middle of the pancake. Fold over from the bottom up, and pinch the edges together by puckering them and pressing them. Beaten egg can be used to help the sealing.

Stuffing
In nonvegetarian cooking, all kinds of meats, fish, and seafoods are commonly used as stuffings. In vegetarian cooking, stuffings most frequently consist of fresh or dried mushrooms, celery, Chinese cabbage, bean curd, spinach, watercress, young leeks, spring onions, braised bamboo shoots, braised bean curd, and red-in-snow. These ingredients, of course, require some seasoning with salt, pepper, soy sauce, sugar, wine, and sesame oil after they have been shredded into broad strips. Fresh and dried mushrooms (the latter previously soaked) must be shredded and stir fried in butter for a couple of minutes. Red-in-snow is usually chopped coarsely and sprinkled in small quantities over the other ingredients to provide greater piquancy.

Cooking
When a sufficient number of these wraplings have been made (allow 6 per person for a snack and 12 each for a meal), brush

them lightly with salad oil, place them on a well-greased surface in a steamer, and steam for 15 minutes. They may also
be boiled, 4 or 5 at a time, in a large pan of boiling water for
10 – 12 minutes.

Serving
Wraplings can be served in soups (like stuffed dumplings), or
they can be served alone, with bowls or dishes of soy sauce
mixed with vinegar on the table for the diners to dip the wraplings in.

The wraplings can also be placed in a well-greased frying
pan or griddle and heated over medium heat for 4 – 5 minutes
until the bottoms are slightly browned. Wraplings cooked in
this way are favorites in Peking, where they are called *kuo
tieh.* In China, the whole family joins in making these wraplings.

WRAPLING STUFFING

A typical bowl of stuffing for 24 wraplings can be made as
follows:

    6 medium-size Chinese dried mushrooms
    3 oz fresh mushrooms
    1 cake bean curd
    2 stalks spring onion
    4 oz Chinese or young savoy cabbage
    4 oz spinach leaf
    1 oz red-in-snow
    ½ tsp salt
    1½ Tb sesame oil
    1½ Tb butter
    1½ Tb soy sauce
    1 tsp sugar
    pepper to taste

Preparation
Soak the dried mushrooms in hot water for ½ hour, discard
stems, and shred into matchsticks. Chop the fresh mushrooms to the same size. Cut the bean curd similarly. Slice the

spring onions into 1-inch segments. Cut the cabbage and spinach into ½-inch slices. Place both vegetables in a large bowl. Chop the red-in-snow coarsely. Sprinkle the vegetables in the bowl with salt, red-in-snow, and sesame oil. Knead with the fingers and leave to absorb seasonings for ½ hour.

Cooking
Heat the butter in a frying pan. Add the spring onions and dried mushrooms. Stir fry together over medium heat for 1½ minutes. Add the bean curd and fresh mushrooms, and sprinkle with soy sauce, sugar, and pepper to taste. Stir fry them together for 2 minutes. Add the contents of the frying pan to the bowl, and mix the 2 groups of ingredients. Use as stuffing for the wraplings.

STEAMED DUMPLINGS (PAOTZE)

These steamed dumplings are much bigger affairs than wraplings; they are about the size of an average orange, but a little squatter in shape, more like mandarins or tangerines. To Westerners, who are used to crisp, brown baked breads, these are a little unusual, because since they are steamed, they are white or cream in color and soft to the touch. Since these dumplings can be eaten cold, they can serve as sandwiches and can be eaten at picnics. As with wraplings, almost anything under the sun can be used as a stuffing for dumplings—so long as it is edible and tasty. Nonvegetarians commonly use cooked meats, vegetables, and seafoods. Vegetarians use the same kinds of stuffing as in wraplings but larger quantities are required for dumplings—3–4 teaspoonfuls for each.

STEAMED DUMPLINGS

For dough skin   *For stuffing*
4¹/₂ cups flour   see under recipe for
¹/₂ tsp salt   Wrapling Stuffing
1¹/₂ tsp baking powder
2 tsp sugar
1¹/₄ cups warm water

Preparation
Sift the flour, salt, baking powder, and sugar into a large bowl. Stir in the water, and mix with a wooden spoon. Form the dough into a ball and allow to stand for ¹/₂ hour. Knead on a well-greased surface, working it thoroughly until it is elastic and bouncy. Cover with damp cloth and leave to develop for 1 hour.

Then form the dough into a roll 2 inches in diameter. Slice off ¹/₂-inch-thick disks and flatten to increase the diameter to approximately 3¹/₂ inches. Make a slight indentation in the center of each disk with the back of a spoon. Place 3–4 teaspoons stuffing in the indentation. Gradually and gently gather the sides of the disk upward until the stuffing is completely covered (as the sides are brought together they should become somewhat creased or puckered). Place each dumpling on a small piece of greased waxed paper.

Cooking
Place the dumplings in a single layer, each on its piece of greased waxed paper, in a steamer, and steam steadily for 30 minutes. Either eat them immediately or serve cold.

You may substitute bean sprouts and watercress for the spinach, and celery for the cabbage, to produce a different stuffing. In the stir frying of the mushrooms and bean curd, a couple of tablespoons of Hot Black-Bean and Tomato Sauce may be added.

For nonvegetarians, 4–5 ounces shredded chicken, pork, lamb, or crabmeat can be added to stir fry with the mushrooms for an extra minute or two. (The bean curd should be omitted.) The meat and mushrooms are then mixed with the vegetables for use as stuffing. The result is highly appetizing.

EGGS

IN EVERY CUISINE in the world, eggs occupy an important place. In somewhat their original form, eggs are usually served in three ways in China: as salted eggs (usually duck eggs), as soy eggs (browned eggs) and as preserved eggs (the "thousand-year-old" variety). All these can be prepared at home, but nowadays, the average Chinese housewife would no more think of making salted and preserved eggs at home than would the average Western housewife think of making butter in her own kitchen. Soy eggs, however, are almost always made at home, probably because they are very easy to do. The three types of eggs are always appetizing when served together in the same dish, if only because of their quite different tastes and colors: the salted egg is white and yellow, the soy egg is brown, and the preserved egg is a yellow-green-and-golden translucent brown. They are most often served for breakfast or midnight supper. Because of their strong flavor, they mate excellently with the blandness of plain rice (usually with congee, or soft rice, or rice gruel). Otherwise, the majority of egg dishes in China are stir fried or steamed.

SOY EGGS

    6 eggs
    ½ cup soy sauce
    ½ cup water or stock
    2 Tb sugar

Preparation
Hard cook the eggs and shell them. Heat the soy sauce, water or stock, and sugar in a saucepan. When it is just about to

boil, lower the eggs into the sauce. Simmer for 25 minutes. Turn off the heat and leave the eggs to cool in the sauce for ¼–½ hour.

Serving
Drain the soy sauce and reserve for other uses. Slice each egg carefully into quarters or sixths, arrange yolk side up on a serving dish.

STEAMED FOUR TYPES OF EGGS

    2 fresh eggs
    1½ cups cold Clear-Simmer Broth
    ½ tsp salt
    pepper to taste
    2 salted eggs
    2 preserved eggs
    2 soy eggs
    1 stalk spring onion
    1½ tsp sesame oil

Preparation
Beat the fresh eggs with a fork for 10 seconds. Add the broth, salt, and pepper, and beat again until well blended. Shell the salted and preserved eggs. Cut each egg into quarters, including the soy eggs. Chop the spring onion coarsely.

Cooking
Arrange the three types of cooked egg, yolk side up, in one layer on a flat, heatproof dish. Pour the beaten egg mixture over them. Place the dish in a steamer, and steam for 15 minutes, by which time the surface of the beaten egg mixture will have jelled. Sprinkle the eggs with the chopped spring onion and sesame oil. Steam for another 2–3 minutes, and serve in the dish. Serves 6–8.

PLAIN STEAMED EGGS

  2 eggs
  2 cups Clear-Simmer Broth
  1 tsp salt
  pepper to taste
  ½ tsp sugar
  1 tsp vegetable oil
  1 Tb sherry
  1 Tb soy sauce
  ½ Tb chopped chives

Preparation and cooking
Beat the eggs, broth, salt, pepper, sugar, and oil together with a fork for 20–30 seconds, until thoroughly blended. Pour the mixture into 2–3-inch-deep heatproof dish. Place the dish in a steamer, and steam for 20 minutes.

Serving
Sprinkle the top of the steamed egg with sherry, soy sauce, and chopped chives, and steam for 1 minute more. Serve in the heatproof dish.

STEAMED EGGS WITH VEGETABLES

The majority of vegetables, which require a comparatively short cooking time, can be steamed with and in the egg and broth mixture of the preceding recipe; vegetables such as spinach, mushrooms, celery, and bean sprouts are commonly used. It is usually best to rub the vegetables with a little salt and oil first and leave them to season for 10 minutes. Then put them on the bottom of the heatproof dish and pour on the beaten egg and broth mixture. The vegetables, singly or in combination, should not exceed in volume ½ that of the egg and broth mixture; otherwise the water they exude when cooked will overpower the eggs, and after all, this is meant to be an egg dish.

Another tangy favorite for sprinkling over the eggs a few

minutes before serving is red-in-snow (1–2 tablespoons chopped coarsely).

For nonvegetarians, there are a number of cooked foods that can be combined with steamed eggs. These include practically all the meats, particularly chopped smoked ham, bacon, roast pork, Chinese sausage, minced beef, and chicken, as well as most fish and seafoods, flaked fish—cod, smoked haddock, etc.—crab, lobster, oyster, shrimp. They can be combined in two ways: either they can be mixed with the beaten egg and broth, or alternatively, they can be stir fried for a short period in a small quantity of oil and used as a garnish. Or the processes can be combined and some of the ingredients can be steamed in the egg and broth mixture, and the rest stir fried and used as garnish. They should be steamed for a minute or two on the egg dish before it is served.

BASIC STIR-FRIED EGGS

2 stalks spring onion	3 Tb vegetable oil
1 tsp salt	1 Tb butter
pepper to taste	1½ Tb sherry
5–6 eggs	

Preparation
Chop the onion into ¼-inch pieces. Add these, along with the salt and pepper, to the eggs. Beat for 10 seconds.

Cooking and Serving
Heat the oil and butter in a frying pan. When hot, lower to medium heat, and add the egg mixture. As the egg begins to set, lift the edges up with a spoon or spatula and draw toward the center, so that the egg on top that is still liquid will flow outward and underneath. Just as the remainder of the eggs is about to set, pour in the sherry from the side. Turn immediately onto a well-heated dish, and serve at once. The addition of a small quantity of sherry at the last moment creates a most appetizing bouquet, which combines with the aroma of the freshly chopped spring onions to give this simple dish its distinction. Serves 5–6.

STIR-FRIED EGGS WITH VEGETABLES

Stir-fried eggs can be combined successfully with a wide range of vegetables, such as spinach, tomatoes, mushrooms, bean sprouts, peas, and green beans. Probably the best way to prepare them is to stir fry the eggs and vegetables in separate frying pans and, at the moment they are both ready, to add the contents of the egg pan to the pan containing the vegetables. The stir-fried eggs should be prepared as in the previous recipe; the vegetables should be stir-fry seasoned with soy sauce and hoisin sauce (1 tablespoon soy sauce, 1/2 tablespoon hoisin sauce, and 1/2 teaspoon sugar to 3/4 pound vegetables, plus 2 tablespoons oil and 1 tablespoon butter). After being stir fried for 2 1/2 – 3 minutes over high heat, the vegetables should be sufficiently cooked, with some gravy left in the pan. When the contents of the egg pan are added to the vegetables and turned and tossed lightly together, the dish should present an attractive contrast between the bright yellow of the eggs and the green, red, brown, or other colors of the vegetables. The contrast between the flavor and texture of the eggs and the vegetables also helps to enhance the appeal of the dish. Just before the dish is served, 1 – 2 teaspoons sesame oil, and 1 extra tablespoon each sherry and soy sauce may be added to the sizzling pan. These increase the distinct aromatic pleasure of the dish.

STIR-FRIED EGGS WITH SPINACH

2 stalks spring onion	3/4 lb spinach
1/2 tsp salt	1 1/2 Tb soy sauce
pepper to taste	1/2 Tb hoisin sauce
4 eggs	1/2 tsp sugar
2 Tb butter	2 Tb sherry
4 Tb vegetable oil	2 tsp sesame oil

Preparation
Use 2 frying pans (if necessary, a saucepan may be used instead of a frying pan for the spinach). Chop the spring onion

into ¼-inch pieces. Add these, along with the salt and pepper, to the eggs. Prepare and cook the eggs in the same manner as in the previous recipe, using butter and 1 tablespoon vegetable oil. Omit the sherry.

Wash and drain the spinach thoroughly. Remove the stems. Save only the unblemished leaves.

Cooking

Heat 3 tablespoons vegetable oil in a frying pan or saucepan over high heat. When the oil is very hot, add the spinach, and turn it briskly in the oil for 2½ minutes. Add the soy sauce, hoisin sauce, and sugar, and continue to stir fry for 1 minute.

Add the contents of the egg pan to the spinach. Stir and turn, keeping the heat high. Add the sherry and sesame oil. Turn once more, and serve. Serves 4–6.

All the other dishes of stir-fried eggs with vegetables can be prepared and cooked in more or less the same manner, stir frying the eggs and vegetables separately, and combining them at the last moment, with the blessing of sherry and sesame oil just before serving.

Sweet-and-Sour Sauce is often poured over stir-fried eggs or plain fried eggs just before serving. The egginess of eggs and the contrasting flavors of the sauce seem to complement each other. Hot Black-Bean and Tomato Sauce can also be used to good effect with most stir-fried egg dishes.

EGG FU-YUNG

In the West, Egg Fu-Yung seems to be applied to all manner of Chinese egg dishes. But in China it is used only for dishes that are produced with beaten egg white cooked with other ingredients (for nonvegetarians, often minced chicken or minced flaked fish is combined and beaten together with the egg white). In Western terms, Egg Fu-Yung should really be called "Chinese egg-white soufflé."

CAULIFLOWER FU-YUNG

　1　medium-size cauliflower
　1　Tb light soy sauce
　4　egg whites
　½　tsp salt
　2　tsp cornstarch
　3　Tb cream
　2　Tb butter
　3　Tb Clear-Simmer Broth
　6　Tb vegetable oil

Preparation

Break the cauliflower into individual flowerets. Parboil for
3 minutes, and drain. Sprinkle evenly with soy sauce. Beat
the egg white with a rotary beater, together with the salt and
cornstarch until nearly stiff but not dry. Add the cream and
continue to mix and beat together for 3–4 seconds.

Cooking

Heat the butter in a saucepan or frying pan. Add the cauliflower and broth. Stir fry over high heat for 2 minutes. Heat
the oil in a frying pan. When hot, reduce the heat to medium,
add the beaten egg white and turn it in the oil until the egg
is set. Drain off the excess oil, and return the pan to the heat.
Pour and fold the contents of the cauliflower pan into the egg
white. Turn and mix gently for 1 minute. Turn out onto a
well-heated dish. Serves 4–6.

GREEN BEANS FU-YUNG

Green beans can be prepared and cooked in the same manner
as Cauliflower Fu-Yung by preparing and stir frying 1 pound
green beans separately from the Fu-Yung. Like the cauliflower in the previous recipe, the green beans will require 3
minutes' parboiling before stir frying. After the stir frying,
combine and fold them into the Fu-Yung for a minute or two
before serving.

For nonvegetarians, the Fu-Yung is often combined with shrimp, crabmeat, flaked fish, or minced chicken and pork. Sometimes these other ingredients are heavily overlaid with quantities of Fu-Yung, so that the shrimp or other seafood appears to be buried in a thick layer of savory white snow!

FLOWING-RUNNING EGGS (LIU HUANG TSAI)

This is an egg dish that is designed to be eaten with rice. Because the dish is smooth, runny, and tasty, it acts as a savory "lubricant" for the rice, often the principal part of a Chinese meal. It is a favorite dish in Peking.

    4 Chinese dried mushrooms
    1 cake bean curd
    2 cloves garlic
    5 eggs
    1/3 tsp salt
    pepper to taste
    3 tsp cornstarch
    1/2 cup Clear-Simmer Broth
    2 1/2 Tb butter
    3 1/2 Tb vegetable oil
    4 Tb green peas
    1/2 Tb sesame oil
    1 1/2 Tb sherry

Preparation
Soak the mushrooms in hot water for 1/2 hour, discard the stems, and cut each mushroom into 6–8 pieces. Chop and mash the bean curd. Crush and chop the garlic. Beat the eggs with a fork for 10 seconds. Add the salt, pepper, cornstarch, and broth. Beat together until well blended and smooth.

Cooking
Melt the butter and 1 tablespoon vegetable oil in a saucepan. When the butter has melted, pour in the egg mixture. Stir slowly but continuously over medium heat with a wooden

spoon until the mixture is quite thick (5–7 minutes). Heat 2½ tablespoons vegetable oil in a small saucepan. Add the garlic and mushrooms and stir fry for 1 minute. Add the green peas, stir, and turn them with the mushrooms for ½ minute. Pour in the mashed bean curd and sesame oil. Stir the contents for 2 minutes. Pour the vegetables into the egg mixture. Stir and mix together for 1 minute. Add the sherry, stir once more, and serve in a bowl. Serves 4–6.

The only difference between the nonvegetarian and the vegetarian version of Flowing-Running Eggs is that in the former, chicken broth is used instead of Clear-Simmer Broth, and 4–5 ounces minced chicken or pork are added to stir fry with the mushrooms for an extra few minutes before they are combined with the other ingredients. When stir frying the mushrooms, peas, and bean curd together, ½ tablespoon light soy sauce can be added.

IRON POT (GROWN) EGGS

The dish was given its name because the eggs "grow" in the iron pot (casserole) during cooking. The dish is in fact a soufflé and can be cooked in a heatproof pyrex glass bowl in the oven.

    2 medium-size tomatoes
    4 large Chinese dried mushrooms
    5 eggs
    1 tsp salt
    2 Tb cornstarch
    1½ tsp baking powder
    ⅔ cup Clear-Simmer Broth
    3 Tb green peas
    ½ Tb sesame oil
    2 Tb grated cheese
    ½ cup milk
    2 Tb clarified butter

Preparation
Skin and dice each tomato into 12 equal cubes. Soak the mushrooms in hot water for ½ hour, discard the stalks, and

cut each mushroom into 6 pieces. Beat the eggs in a bowl with a rotary beater for 10 seconds. Add all the other ingredients, and beat for a further 20 seconds. Preheat oven to 350 degrees.

Cooking and Serving
Pour the egg mixture into a large well-greased heatproof dish; it should fill only one-third of the depth to leave room for expansion. Place the dish in a preheated oven at 350 degrees for 30–35 minutes. During that time, the eggs should have "grown" or expanded two- or threefold—in other words, risen like a soufflé. The dish must be served and eaten before it collapses.

TEA EGGS

6–8 eggs
water for boiling
3 Tb Indian tea
1 Tb salt
3 cups water

Preparation
Hard cook the eggs gently, for 8–9 minutes. Cool in the water. When cool tap carefully with a spoon to crack the entire surface of the shells without chipping off any pieces.

Cooking and Serving
Heat the 3 cups water in a saucepan. When it boils, add the tea and salt. Stir and immerse the cooked eggs in the salted tea. Leave to simmer very gently for ½ hour. Turn the heat off and leave the eggs to stand in the tea for 2 hours.

Pour off the tea, drain the eggs, and shell when cool. Slice each egg lengthwise into quarters and serve for breakfast, late supper, or as a snack at any time.

BEAN CURD

BEAN CURD (*tofu*) is one of the basic foods of the Chinese, as it is of the Japanese. It is a cream-colored, custardlike, slightly spongy substance, generally sold in shops (in almost every Chinese food store and supermarket) in cakes of about 2½–3 inches square and 1 inch thick. In itself it is fairly bland in taste—and therefore not necessarily immediately appealing to the average Western palate—but it is perfectly suited to absorb other tastes and flavors and can be cooked with almost every known food, fish, flesh, fowl, or vegetable. Cooked in some such combination, it becomes, to the Chinese and Japanese at least, a welcome accompaniment to rice. For connoisseurs, even the very blandness of the bean curd is attractive. It has long been prized for its high protein value.

COLD BEAN CURD

    4 cakes bean curd
    4 cups water
    2½ Tb soy sauce
    2 Tb peanut oil

Preparation and Cooking
Cut each bean curd into 4 pieces. Place them in a wire basket. Immerse in boiling water and simmer for 3 minutes. Drain. Place the pieces of bean curd on a serving dish. Blend the soy sauce with the peanut oil and pour the mixture over the bean curd. For variation, a small amount of chili oil (or 1–1½ teaspoons chili sauce) may be blended with the soy sauce and peanut-oil mixture. Serves 4–6.

For nonvegetarians add 1 tablespoon shrimp sauce or oyster sauce to the preceding mixture.

COLD BEAN CURD WITH SESAME PASTE OR PEANUT BUTTER

Repeat the previous recipe. Use 1½ tablespoons sesame paste or 2 tablespoons peanut butter mixed with 2 teaspoons sesame oil, and blend the mixture with the soy sauce and peanut oil.

HOT-AND-SAVORY BEAN-CURD PUDDING

This is a west Chinese, Szechuan dish, called Ma-Po Tofu.

    4 cakes bean curd
    1 medium-size green pepper
    1 – 2 chili peppers
    ¾ Tb salted black beans
    6 medium-size Chinese dried mushrooms
    2 cloves garlic
    3 Tb vegetable oil
    2 Tb butter
    2 tsp soybean paste
    2 Tb soy sauce
    1 tsp red or cream bean-curd cheese
    1 Tb hoisin sauce
    1 – 2 tsp chili sauce
    1 Tb tomato purée
    1 tsp sugar
    1 Tb sherry
    3 tsp cornstarch

Preparation
Cut each bean-curd cake into 12 pieces. Cut the green pepper and the chili pepper into ¼-inch pieces, discarding seeds. Soak the black beans in 1 cup water for 15 minutes, drain, and mash. Soak the mushrooms in 1 cup hot water for ½ hour. Drain, reserving water, remove stems, and chop coarsely. Crush and chop the garlic.

Cooking

Heat the oil in a frying pan. Add the peppers, mushrooms, and garlic, and stir fry over medium heat for 3–4 minutes. Add the butter and all the other ingredients except the bean curd and the cornstarch. Continue to stir fry for another 3–4 minutes. Mix the cornstarch with 4 tablespoons mushroom water. Add to pan and stir quickly to blend with the other ingredients. Finally add the bean curd. Turn and stir it in the bubbling sauce, until it is well heated through, and all of it is well covered and mixed with the sauce. This dish is greatly appreciated by rice eaters. Serves 6–8.

For nonvegetarians, add ¼–½ pound minced pork or chicken with the garlic, black beans, and pepper in the initial stir frying, and extend the cooking time by a couple of minutes.

HOT-AND-PUNGENT BEAN-CURD PUDDING

In this variation of the previous recipe, three extra flavoring ingredients are added: 1½ tablespoons chopped hot-pickled Szechuan greens, 2 tablespoons vinegar, and 1½ tablespoons red-in-snow. When the red-in-snow is coarsely minced for sprinkling over the bean curd just before serving, it dramatically changes the flavor and character of the dish. The hot-pickled greens and the vinegar should be added at the beginning of the second stage of the stir frying, along with the butter.

RED-COOKED BEAN CURD WITH BEAN-CURD STICKS

Bean-curd sticks are about 20 inches long. They have a glossy, lacquerlike surface and are creamy in color. Since they are hard, they must be soaked before using.

    3 cakes bean curd
    2 lily-bud stems
    3 bean-curd sticks
    6 medium-size Chinese dried mushrooms
    1 stalk spring onion
    2 cloves garlic
    2 slices ginger root
    2 Tb vegetable oil
    1 Tb butter
    1 tsp soybean paste
    2½ Tb soy sauce
    1 tsp chili sauce
    1 tsp sugar
    1 Tb hoisin sauce
    1½ cups Vegetable Broth
    1 Tb tomato purée
    2 Tb sherry

Preparation
Cut each bean-curd cake into 6 pieces. Soak the lily buds and bean-curd sticks for 1 hour in warm water. Drain, and cut into 2-inch pieces. Soak the dried mushrooms in 1 cup hot water for ½ hour. Drain, discard the stems, and cut each mushroom into halves or quarters, depending on size. Reserve the water. Cut the spring onion into 1-inch pieces. Crush the garlic and shred the ginger.

Cooking
Heat the oil and butter in a casserole. Add the garlic, ginger, and half the spring onion. Stir fry for ½ minute. Add the mushrooms, lily buds, and bean-curd sticks. Stir fry together for 3 minutes. Add all the rest of the ingredients except the bean curd and the sherry. Bring to a boil and simmer very

gently for ½ hour. Add 4–5 tablespoons mushroom water and 1 tablespoon sherry, and mix with the sauce until well blended. Add all the bean-curd pieces. Turn and mix them in the sauce and other ingredients. Cover and place an asbestos pad under the casserole; simmer for 15 minutes. Sprinkle with the rest of the sherry and spring onion and serve in the casserole.

For nonvegetarians, add ½–1 pound red-cooked meat—pork or beef—to cook with the bean curd during the last ½ hour.

STIR-FRIED BEAN CURDS

Bean curds can be stir fried with almost any kind of vegetable that is traditionally stir fried. When making such dishes, it is customary to stir fry the vegetables with ingredients that will produce a good quantity of sauce or gravy, which is in turn absorbed by the bean curd during the final phase of stir frying together, producing a highly savory dish.

BEAN CURD STIR FRIED WITH BEAN SPROUTS OR SPINACH

3 cakes bean curd
3 stalks spring onion
3 large Chinese dried mushrooms
2 cloves garlic
1 slice ginger root
3 Tb vegetable oil
1 tsp soybean paste
2 Tb soy sauce
½ Tb hoisin sauce
1 tsp chili sauce
1 tsp sugar
4 Tb Vegetable Broth
1½ Tb butter
1 Tb sherry
½ lb bean sprouts or spinach

Preparation
Cut each bean curd into 6–8 pieces. Cut the spring onions into 1-inch segments. Soak the mushrooms in hot water for ½ hour, discard the stems, and shred into matchsticks. Crush the garlic and shred the ginger.

Cooking
Heat the oil in a frying pan. Add garlic, ginger, and half the spring onion, and stir fry over medium heat for ½ minute. Add the soybean paste, soy sauce, hoisin sauce, chili sauce, sugar, and Vegetable Broth. Stir fry them together for 2 minutes. Add the bean curd. Turn and stir in the sauce until well covered and heated through. Remove bean curd and set aside, keeping hot. Add butter and sherry. Raise heat to its highest. Add the bean sprouts to the pan, and mix and turn quickly in the bubbling sauce and oil for 2 minutes. Add the remaining spring onions, and return the bean curd to the pan. Turn and stir the contents for 1 minute and serve. Eat immediately as the "heat effect" is an important part of the dish's flavor. If spinach is used instead of bean sprouts, only the tender leaves should be chosen, and the amount of butter should be increased by 1 tablespoon.

BEAN CURD STIR FRIED WITH GREEN BEANS

Repeat the previous recipe, using green beans instead of bean sprouts. Trim the ends of the beans and parboil for 3–4 minutes. Then stir fry, for about 1 minute longer than for the bean sprouts. Then return the bean curd to the pan for the final stir frying.

In either of the two recipes above the bean curd can also be simply stir fried once, placed in the center of a hot serving dish, and later surrounded by the vegetables after they have been stir fried. If that is done, the stir frying of the bean curd should be extended by 1 minute. Alternatively, the bean curd can be deep fried first for 2 minutes and drained before being stir fried. Which method you choose at this stage is a matter of personal taste and inclination.

For nonvegetarians, ¼ – ½ pound minced pork is usually added to the initial stir frying, which will then require a few extra minutes. The amounts of all the seasonings and flavorers should be increased by one-quarter. For more elaborate dishes, shrimp and crabmeat can be used instead of minced pork or in conjunction with it in the initial stir frying.

DEEP-FRIED BEAN CURD STIR FRIED WITH DUCK EGGS AND CUCUMBER SKINS

3 cakes bean curd
oil for deep frying
3 hard-cooked duck eggs
6-inch segment cucumber
1 medium-sized onion
1 clove garlic
3 Tb vegetable oil
2 tsp red bean-curd cheese
1 Tb light soy sauce
4 Tb Vegetable Broth
pepper to taste
2 Tb sherry
2 Tb butter
½ Tb dark soy sauce
½ Tb hoisin sauce
½ tsp sugar
2 tsp vinegar

Preparation
Cut each bean curd into 6 – 8 pieces. Deep fry for 2 minutes, and drain. Chop the duck eggs coarsely. Cut the unpeeled cucumber into 3 equal pieces. Slice each piece vertically into 8 pieces, each piece having some green skin. Cut the onion into very thin slices. Crush the garlic.

Cooking

Heat vegetable oil in a frying pan. Add the garlic and onion.
Stir fry for 1½ minutes. Add the eggs, bean-curd cheese,
light soy sauce, broth, pepper to taste, and sherry. Turn and
stir for ½ minute. Add the bean curd. Mix and stir the pieces
for 2 minutes with the egg and sauce. Pour out onto the center of a well-heated serving dish.

Heat the butter in a separate frying pan. Add in the cucumber, the dark soy sauce, hoisin sauce, sugar, and vinegar. Stir
fry for 1½ minutes. Spoon the cucumber around the bean
curd and duck eggs at the center of the serving dish.

DEEP-FRIED BEAN CURD STIR FRIED WITH EGGS, MUSHROOMS, AND WOOD EARS

    3 cakes bean curd
    3 eggs
    4 medium-size Chinese dried mushrooms
    2 Tb wood ears
    2 stalks spring onion
    oil for deep frying
    3 Tb vegetable oil
    1½ Tb soy sauce
    ½ Tb hoisin sauce
    1 tsp sugar
    4 Tb Vegetable Broth
    2 Tb butter
    ½ tsp salt
    pepper to taste
    2 Tb sherry
    ½ Tb sesame oil

Preparation

Cut each piece of bean curd into 6 pieces. Beat eggs lightly
for 10 seconds. Soak mushrooms in 1 cup warm water for ½
hour. Reserve water. Discard the stems, and shred the mushrooms into strips. Soak the wood ears in warm water for ½

hour, rinse, and clean thoroughly. Cut the spring onions into 1-inch segments. Deep fry the bean curd for 2–3 minutes and drain.

Cooking

Heat the oil in a frying pan. Add the mushrooms and wood ears, and stir fry for 1 minute over medium heat. Add the soy sauce, hoisin sauce, sugar, broth, and 3 tablespoons mushroom water. Continue to heat and stir for 2 minutes. Add the pieces of bean curd. Turn them to mix with the mushrooms and wood ears for 2 minutes, until well covered with sauce.

In another frying pan, melt the butter over medium heat, add the spring onion, and pour in the beaten egg. Tilt and shake the pan so that the egg covers the bottom of the pan evenly. As soon as the egg has hardened, break it up into ½-inch pieces. Sprinkle with the salt and pepper. Pour in the sherry. Turn the egg over once, and add it to the pan containing the bean curd, mushrooms, and wood ears. Turn and mix them once together over medium heat, pour the contents onto a serving dish, sprinkle with sesame oil, and serve. Not only is this dish aromatic, but the combination of the black of the mushrooms and wood ears with the yellow of the egg, the green of the onion, and the brown of the bean curd makes an appealing array of colors.

In its nonvegetarian version, ¼–½ pound thinly sliced lean pork is stir fried in oil for a couple of minutes before the mushrooms and wood ears are added. After 3–4 minutes of cooking together with slightly increased quantities of seasonings and flavorers, and later with bean curd added, the contents are combined with the stir-fried eggs. The mixture gains aroma by the last-minute addition of sesame oil and sherry. This is a well-known Peking dish called Mu Shu Jou. In the south even greater savoriness is obtained by adding 2–3 ounces oysters or mussels to the stir frying with the pork.

STIR-FRIED SHREDDED BEAN CURD WITH DRIED BAMBOO SHOOTS, DRIED MUSHROOMS, LILY-BUD STEMS, AND SEAWEED

  3 cakes bean curd
  2 stalks spring onion
  2 lily-bud stems
  3 oz Chinese dried bamboo shoots
  3 oz Chinese dried mushrooms
  3 oz seaweed (hair type, optional)
  4 Tb vegetable oil
  2 Tb sherry
  1 Tb butter
  1 tsp cream bean-curd cheese
  1 Tb light soy sauce
  2 Tb Clear-Simmer Broth
  1 Tb sesame oil
  1 Tb dark soy sauce
  ½ Tb hoisin sauce
  6 Tb Vegetable Broth
  ½ tsp sugar
  1 tsp chili sauce
  1½ tsp cornstarch (blended
      in 2 Tb mushroom water)

Preparation
Cut the bean curd into ¼-inch-wide strips the length of a matchstick. Cut the spring onions and lily-bud stems into 2-inch segments, soak in warm water for 1 hour, and drain. Soak the dried bamboo shoots in warm water for 1 hour. Shred into matchsticks. Soak mushrooms in 1 cup warm water for ½ hour. Reserve water. Shred mushrooms also into matchsticks, discarding stalks. Soak the seaweed for 1 hour, changing water twice. Rub with 2 teaspoons oil and 2 teaspoons sherry, and let stand for ½ hour.

Cooking

Heat 2 tablespoons vegetable oil and the butter in a frying pan. Add the lily-bud stems to stir fry over medium heat for 2 minutes. Add the spring onions, bean-curd cheese, light soy sauce, and Clear-Simmer Broth. Continue to stir fry for 1 minute. Add the bean-curd strips, turn them in the sauce to mix with the lily buds and spring onions, and simmer gently for another 2 minutes.

In another pan, heat 1½ tablespoons vegetable oil with the sesame oil. Add the shredded dried bamboo shoots, shredded mushrooms, and seaweed. Stir fry for 2 minutes. Add all the remaining ingredients except the cornstarch. Stir fry for 2 minutes. Finally add the cornstarch and mushroom-water mixture, and continue to stir fry for 2 minutes. Pour the contents of one pan into the other. Toss and turn until the strips are evenly mixed.

Pour the contents onto a heatproof serving dish. Place the dish in a steamer and steam for 15 minutes.

CLEAR-SIMMERED BEAN CURDS

Bean curds are traditionally cooked in China either with a very savory sauce (as illustrated in the previous recipes) or by simmering in a clear broth with not more than 1 or 2 vegetable ingredients. This produces a dish that is distinctive for its purity and its undisguised presentation of the native flavors of the principal ingredients. It provides a welcome contrast to the distinctive tastes of the majority of the other dishes on the table — which in the Chinese meal usually means a buffet with 4 or 6 or more dishes.

CLEAR-SIMMERED BEAN CURD WITH LETTUCE AND CELLOPHANE NOODLES

    4 cakes bean curd
    ½ lb lettuce
    2 oz cellophane noodles
    3 cups Clear-Simmer Broth
    1 tsp salt
    ½ Tb light soy sauce
    pepper to taste
    1 tsp sesame oil

Preparation
Cut each piece of bean curd into quarters. Clean the lettuce thoroughly, discarding any discolored leaves, and cut away the base and tougher parts of the stem. Cut each leaf in half slantwise across the stem. Soak the noodles in warm water for 10 minutes, and drain.

Cooking
Place the lettuce and bean curd, together with all the other ingredients and broth, in a heatproof glass bowl. Steam for ½ hour. Serve.

CLEAR-SIMMERED BEAN CURD WITH BEAN SPROUTS, WATER CHESTNUTS, AND SLICED CUCUMBERS

    4 cakes bean curd
    ¼ lb bean sprouts
    ½ medium-size cucumber
    3 water chestnuts
    3 cups Clear-Simmer Broth
    1 tsp salt
    ½ Tb light soy sauce
    ½ Tb yeast extract
    pepper to taste
    1 tsp sesame oil

Preparation
Cut each piece of bean curd into quarters. Thoroughly rinse and wash the bean sprouts, which must be very fresh and plump. Wash the cucumber, leaving skin on, and cut lengthwise into pieces twice the size of mah-jongg tiles (about 2 inches by 1 inch by ½ inch). Each piece should have some skin. Cut each water chestnut into 4 – 6 slices.

Cooking
Place all the ingredients in a heatproof bowl, pouring the broth on top. Place the bowl in a steamer, and steam for ½ hour. Serve in the bowl.

For nonvegetarians, add 1 tablespoon dried shrimp parboiled for 2 minutes and 2 tablespoons fresh shrimp. If the dish tastes too fishy, 1 – 2 slices of ginger root and 1 tablespoon sherry may be added.

Before we conclude this section on *tofu*, or bean curd, it is worth noting that during elaborate Buddhist banquets (which must be vegetarian), imitation poultry, fish, and meats are served, often looking very like the real thing. The basic material used to achieve this craftsmanship is always bean curd, along with bean-curd skin and bean-curd sticks. The usual meat dishes that are simulated in vegetarian food are the red-cooked ones, since bean curd and its by-products, when braised or fried with soy sauce and soybean paste, become almost precisely the same color as meat, fish, or poultry that has been similarly cooked. When used in layers, bean-curd skin also has the appearance and texture of the flaking flesh of fish or poultry that has been marinaded and deep fried. The white meat of chicken or the under-layer flesh of fish or pork that has not been touched by soy can be imitated by the creamy softness of uncolored bean curd or bean-curd skins used in layers.

The legs, claws, and crests of birds, and the tails of fish, can be made from bean-curd sticks cut and shaped with scissors after soaking. Such reconstructions of birds, fish, and meat are made for the diners to marvel at. Endeavors like these, however, are really more handcraft than cooking, and since any effort at a similar achievement would take days or weeks of patient labor, I would not recommend that the average housewife try them. This is an activity best left to the monks in their cells and their usually vast open-plan kitchens, where work starts at 3 A.M. and thought is directed toward achieving perfection rather than toward cooking the family's meal. For us who are more materially grounded, it is best to direct our energy into areas where maximum results can be achieved with minimum effort, even though we are dealing with a cuisine whose traditions and techniques are derived in the main from a more leisured past.

CHINESE COLD SALADS

ALTHOUGH WE CHINESE seldom eat anything raw, and our cuisine has no great salad tradition, we do make a number of interesting salad dishes that can be produced in the modern kitchen and used to supplement the usual Western range of salads.

The number of portions is not given for the salads, as they can be served as a main or a side dish.

CHINESE CARROT SALAD

1½ lb young carrots	2 Tb soy sauce
3 tsp salt	2 Tb vinegar
1 Tb sugar	1 Tb sesame oil

Preparation
Scrape and clean the carrots thoroughly. Cut them diagonally into very thin slices. Cut each slice again into six strips. Parboil for 2 minutes and drain. Sprinkle with salt and rub it thoroughly into the carrot strips. Let stand for 1½ hours; pour off all the water that has been extracted by the salt. Rinse quickly under running water, and drain and dry on paper towels.

Flavoring and Serving
Place the carrot strips in a salad bowl. Sprinkle with sugar, soy sauce, vinegar, and sesame oil. Toss them together a few times and serve either on their own or with other ingredients in a mixed salad.

CABBAGE AND CELERY MUSTARD SALAD

In China, we would customarily use Chinese cabbage for this salad. In the West, where Chinese cabbage is not always available, it might be best to use a mixture of savoy cabbage and celery or lettuce.

    1 lb young savoy cabbage
    ³/₄ lb celery or lettuce
    1 ½ Tb mustard powder
    2 Tb soy sauce
    ½ tsp salt
    1 Tb wine vinegar
    1 tsp chili sauce
    1 Tb sherry
    1 ½ Tb vegetable oil
    ½ Tb sesame oil

Preparation
Clean the vegetables thoroughly. Cut away the roots and unsightly parts, and break into individual leaves or stems. Cut the celery and the cabbage diagonally into 2-inch pieces. Plunge them into a large pan of boiling water and parboil for 3 minutes. Drain and place in a casserole. Mix the mustard in a bowl with 2–3 tablespoons water, stir into a paste, add the soy sauce, salt, vinegar, chili sauce, and sherry. Stir until well blended.

Serving
While the vegetables in the casserole are still hot, spoon the mustard mixture evenly over them. Toss and stir them together with vegetable oil and sesame oil until well mixed. Cover the casserole and heat for 1 minute. Turn off the heat, remove cover, and cool. Serve either in the casserole or in a salad bowl.

CHINESE SALAD

1½ lb romaine lettuce
¼ lb young carrots
4 medium-size tomatoes
½ lb bean sprouts
¾ Tb chopped chives
1 medium-size onion
3 cloves garlic
2 slices ginger root
3 Tb vegetable oil
2 Tb Vegetable Broth
2 Tb soy sauce
1 Tb hoisin sauce
1½ Tb sherry
1 Tb sesame oil

Preparation
Clean the lettuce, remove the base, and cut or tear the leaves into 2–3-inch pieces. Slice the carrots into matchsticks. The tomatoes must be fresh and firm. Skin them and cut each into quarters. Wash and rinse the bean sprouts, which must be fresh and plump, and drain thoroughly. Chop the chives and onion coarsely. Crush the garlic, shred the ginger, and chop both into coarse grains. Heat the oil in a small pan. When hot, add the onion, garlic, and ginger. Stir fry for 1 minute. Add the broth. Stir 2–3 times, and turn off the heat. Mix the soy sauce, hoisin sauce, sherry, and sesame oil in a bowl. Pour the contents of the pan into the bowl and mix all ingredients together until well blended.

Serving
Place the vegetables in a salad bowl. Sprinkle the flavorers in the other bowl over them. Toss until well mixed. Sprinkle with chives and serve.

BEAN-SPROUT AND BAMBOO-SHOOT SALAD

    8 oz bamboo shoots
    4 oz canned braised bamboo shoots
    1 lb bean sprouts
    2 stalks spring onion
    3 slices ginger root
    2 cloves garlic
    2 Tb Vegetable Broth
    2 Tb soy sauce
    ¾ Tb hoisin sauce
    1 tsp chili oil
    1 Tb sherry
    2 Tb vegetable oil
    ¾ Tb sesame oil

Preparation
Keeping them separate, slice both types of bamboo shoots
into strips the length of a matchstick and twice as wide.
Wash and rinse the bean sprouts, which must be fresh and
plump. Parboil for 2 minutes, and drain thoroughly. Parboil
the 8 ounces bamboo shoots for 4 minutes, and drain. Chop
the spring onions into ⅛-inch pieces. Shred the ginger,
crush the garlic, and chop both coarsely. Place them in a
bowl, and add all the other seasoning and flavoring ingredients. Mix until well blended.

Serving
Put the bamboo shoots and bean sprouts in a salad bowl.
Sprinkle the blended mixture from the other bowl evenly
over them. Toss and serve.

ASPARAGUS, BAMBOO-SHOOT, AND CUCUMBER SALAD

1 bunch asparagus
6 oz bamboo shoots
6-inch piece cucumber
2 Tb soy sauce
1 Tb hoisin sauce
2 Tb Vegetable Broth
1 tsp chili sauce
1½ Tb vegetable oil
¾ Tb sesame oil
2 Tb sherry

Preparation
Remove the base and tougher end of the asparagus. Divide each remaining piece in half lengthwise. Cut again into 3-inch segments. Parboil for 4–5 minutes, and drain thoroughly. Cut the bamboo shoots into pieces of the same size. Parboil for 5–6 minutes, and drain. Cut the cucumber in half lengthwise, and then again into 3-inch slivers.

Mix all the seasoning and flavoring ingredients in a bowl until well blended.

Serving
Place the three vegetables in a salad bowl. Pour the blended mixture from the other bowl over them. Toss and chill for 30 minutes in the refrigerator.

THE THREE FAIRY SALAD

1½ lb Chinese cabbage or lettuce
4 oz radishes
1½ Tb salt
1 medium-size onion
2 chili peppers
3 Tb vegetable oil
3 tsp sesame oil
2 Tb coarsely chopped coriander leaves

Preparation

Clean the cabbage thoroughly, discard the base, and cut the leaves into 1½–2-inch pieces. Chop the radishes and mix with the cabbage. Sprinkle with salt and work it gently into them. Leave to season for 3 hours. Sprinkle with 1 cup water. Drain and dry vegetables thoroughly on paper towels. Slice the onion into thin slices. Chop the peppers, discarding the seeds.

Heat the vegetable oil in a small frying pan. Stir fry the onion and pepper over medium heat for 3 minutes, then discard. Add the sesame oil to the remaining oil in the pan.

Serving

Sprinkle the blended oil over the radishes and cabbage. Toss and sprinkle with chopped coriander.

EIGHT PRECIOUS SALAD

¼ bowl wood ears
¼ bowl Chinese dried mushrooms
¼ bowl lily-bud stems
¼ bowl shredded bean-curd skin
6 Tb vegetable oil
1 bowl shredded carrots
¼ bowl shredded turnips
1 bowl bean sprouts
½ bowl shredded bamboo shoots
2 Tb Vegetable Broth
1 Tb sesame oil
½ tsp salt
2 Tb soy sauce
½ Tb hoisin sauce
1½ Tb vinegar

Preparation

Soak the wood ears and mushrooms in hot water for ½ hour. Cut the mushrooms into strips, discarding stems. Rinse and clean the wood ears thoroughly. Soak the lily-bud stems and bean-curd skin in warm water for 2 hours, and drain. Cut both into approximately 2-inch segments.

Heat 3 tablespoons vegetable oil in a saucepan. Add the carrots and turnips, and stir fry for 3 minutes. Add the bean sprouts and bamboo shoots, and continue to stir fry for 2 minutes.

Heat the other 3 tablespoons vegetable oil in another saucepan. Add the lily-bud stems, mushrooms, and bean-curd skin, and stir fry together for 3 minutes. Add the wood ears, and continue to stir fry for 2 minutes. In a separate bowl, mix the broth with the sesame oil and all the other seasoning and flavoring ingredients.

Serving
Mix the two groups of stir-fried vegetables in a large salad bowl. Sprinkle with the blended mixture from the other bowl. Toss and serve hot or cold.

For nonvegetarians, in China shredded roast duck or chicken meat and a few teaspoons of shrimp oil are often added to any of the above salads.

CHINESE HOT SALADS

As THE NAME SUGGESTS, a hot salad differs from an ordinary one in that it is served and eaten hot. The essence of the hot salad is fresh crispness combined with heat, achieved by tossing the main vegetable briefly in hot oil and flavoring ingredients and sauces. Stir frying is used in preparing these hot salads, but here it is an even swifter process than ordinary quick stir frying. This method, which is an integral part of the Chinese way of preparing vegetables, can prove a very useful addition to the average Western kitchen.

HOT SWEET-PEPPER AND BAMBOO-SHOOT SALAD

2 Tb soy sauce
1 Tb hoisin sauce
1½ Tb sherry
2 tsp sugar
1½ tsp chili sauce
2 large red sweet peppers
2 large green sweet peppers
5–6 oz bamboo shoots
3–4 oz canned braised bamboo shoots
2 Tb corn oil
1½ Tb butter
1½ Tb sesame oil

Preparation
Mix the first 5 ingredients — the flavorers — in a bowl. Chop the peppers and bamboo shoots into matchsticks.

Cooking and Serving
Heat the corn oil, butter, and sesame oil in a large saucepan or frying pan. When very hot, add the shredded vegetables and turn and toss for ½ minute. Pour the flavoring ingredients evenly over the vegetables. Continue to turn and toss and stir fry for ½ minute.

Serve on a well-heated serving dish and eat immediately. The rapid turning and tossing of the vegetables in hot oil creates a very bright, flavorful, aromatic dish.

HOT BEAN-SPROUT, BAMBOO-SHOOT, AND MUSHROOM SALAD

2 oz Chinese dried mushrooms
1 lb fresh bean sprouts
4 oz bamboo shoots
2 stalks spring onion
2 Tb soy sauce
1½ tsp sugar
2 Tb dry sherry
2 tsp mustard
¾ Tb hoisin sauce
2 Tb corn oil
1½ Tb butter
1 Tb sesame oil

Preparation
Soak the dried mushrooms in hot water for ½ hour. Discard the stems and shred the mushrooms into matchsticks. Shred the bamboo shoots and bean sprouts in the same way. Cut the spring onions (including the green parts) into 2½-inch pieces. Mix the soy sauce, sugar, sherry, mustard, and hoisin sauce in a bowl.

Cooking and Serving

Heat the corn oil, butter, and sesame oil in a large saucepan or frying pan. When it is very hot, add the mushrooms. Stir fry over high heat for ¼ minute. Add all the other vegetables. Continue to stir fry rapidly for ½ minute. Pour the flavoring ingredients from the bowl evenly over the vegetables. Stir fry for a further ½ minute, and serve on a well-heated serving dish.

HOT SPINACH AND BAMBOO-SHOOT SALAD

    1½ lb fresh leaf spinach
    ½ lb canned bamboo shoots
    1½ Tb butter
    salt and pepper to taste
    3 Tb corn oil
    2½ Tb soy sauce
    1½ tsp sugar
    1 Tb sesame oil

Preparation

Clean the spinach thoroughly. Cut away and discard all the coarser stems and leaves. Cut the bamboo shoots into strips ¼ inch thick.

Cooking and Serving

Heat the butter in a small frying pan over medium heat. Add the bamboo shoots. Sprinkle them with salt and pepper to taste and stir fry for ½ minute. Heat the corn oil in a large saucepan until it is very hot. Add the spinach and turn rapidly in the oil for ¾ minute over high heat. Sprinkle the soy sauce and sugar evenly over the spinach and continue to stir fry for a further ¼ minute. Add the buttered bamboo shoots and sesame oil to the spinach. Stir fry the two vegetables together, still over high heat, for a further ½ minute, and serve.

    The dark green of the spinach and the ivory whiteness of the bamboo shoots make an attractive contrast in color as well as in texture.

HOT MUSHROOM AND ASPARAGUS SALAD

    1 bunch asparagus
    2 Tb butter
    ¼ lb Chinese dried mushrooms
    1 lb fresh mushrooms
    2 Tb corn oil
    1 Tb sesame oil
    1½ Tb soy sauce
    1 Tb soybean paste
    1 Tb hoisin sauce
    2 Tb dry sherry
    1 tsp sugar

Preparation and Cooking

Remove the base and tougher ends of the asparagus. Chop the rest into pieces ¼–½ inch thick. Parboil for 3 minutes in a big pot of boiling water. Drain the water, add the butter, and toss the asparagus over medium heat for 1½ minutes. Soak the Chinese dried mushrooms for ½ hour in 1 cup warm water. Retain 3 tablespoons mushroom water, discard the stems of the mushrooms, and slice the tops into ¼-inch-thick strips. Discard the stems of the fresh mushrooms, and slice them into strips of the same size. Heat the corn oil and sesame oil in a saucepan. When hot, add both kinds of mushrooms, and stir fry for 1 minute over high heat. Add the butter, asparagus, and the rest of the ingredients. Continue to stir fry and toss for ½ minute, and serve.

HOT CABBAGE, CARROT, AND RADISH SALAD

    1 lb white cabbage
    1/2 lb young carrots
    3 large radishes
    3–4 tsp salt
    1 Tb soy sauce
    2 tsp sugar
    1 1/2 Tb wine vinegar
    1 Tb sherry
    2 tsp mustard powder
    2 Tb corn oil
    2 Tb butter

Preparation
Shred all three vegetables into 1/4-inch-thick strips. Sprinkle and rub with salt, and leave to season for 2 hours. Drain off any water that accumulates. Mix the remaining ingredients — except for the oil and butter — in a bowl.

Cooking and Serving
Heat the oil and butter in a large saucepan. When very hot, add all the shredded vegetables, and stir fry over high heat for 1 minute. Add the ingredients from the bowl, continue to toss and stir fry for 1 minute longer, and serve.

HOT LETTUCE AND CABBAGE SALAD WITH SWEET-AND-SOUR SAUCE

    1 lb white or Chinese cabbage
    1 head romaine or leaf lettuce
    6–8 Tb Sweet-and-Sour Sauce
    2 Tb corn oil
    1 Tb sesame oil
    1 Tb butter

Preparation

Remove the roots of the vegetables. Cut each leaf slantwise into 2–3 pieces. Prepare the Sweet-and-Sour Sauce, and keep warm in a small pan.

Cooking and Serving

Heat the corn oil, sesame oil, and butter in a large saucepan. When hot, add the cabbage, and turn and stir fry over high heat for 1½ minutes. Add the lettuce and stir fry the two vegetables together for ½ minute. Pour the Sweet-and-Sour Sauce over the vegetables. Turn and toss them in the sauce for 25 seconds longer, and serve.

CELERY AND CUCUMBER SALAD WITH BEETS

¼ – ½ lb beets
1 medium-size cucumber
1 bunch celery (about ¾ lb)
1½ Tb soy sauce
1 Tb hoisin sauce
2 tsp sugar
1 Tb wine vinegar
1 Tb dry sherry
1½ tsp chili sauce
1 Tb butter
2 Tb corn or peanut oil
1 Tb sesame oil

Preparation

Trim the beets and cut into strips ¼ inch thick. Clean the cucumber (retaining the skin) and celery thoroughly, and slice into the same size strips. Mix and toss the vegetables together. Mix the rest of the ingredients – except for the butter and oils – in a bowl.

Cooking and Serving
Heat the butter and oils in a large saucepan or frying pan.
When very hot, add all vegetables and stir fry rapidly over
high heat for 1 minute. Sprinkle the ingredients from the
bowl evenly over the vegetables, and continue to toss, turn,
and stir fry for 1 minute. Then serve.

CHINESE EGG, MUSHROOM, AND SPRING-ONION HOT SALAD

    3 eggs
    ½ tsp salt
    pepper to taste
    3 Tb butter
    ½ lb mushrooms
    5–6 stalks spring onion
    1½ Tb soy sauce
    1 tsp chili sauce
    2 Tb dry sherry
    1½ tsp sugar
    1½ Tb corn or peanut oil
    1½ Tb sesame oil

Preparation
Beat the eggs lightly with the salt and pepper. Melt 2 tablespoons butter in a frying pan, and make a very thin omelet
with the beaten egg. When the omelet is cool, slice into very
thin strips double the length of matchsticks or longer. Wash
and rinse the mushrooms thoroughly, discard the stems, and
slice caps into thin strips. Chop the spring onions into 2½-
inch segments. Mix the soy sauce, chili sauce, sherry, and
sugar in a bowl.

Cooking and Serving
Heat remaining butter and the oils in a large frying pan or
saucepan. When hot, add the shredded mushrooms. Toss and
stir fry for ½ minute over high heat. Add the spring onions

and shredded omelet, stir fry, and turn for ½ minute. Sprinkle the ingredients from the bowl evenly over the contents of the pan. Toss, turn, and stir fry for ½ minute longer. Serve.

CHINESE HOT-RICE SALAD

3 Soy Eggs
3–4 oz Chinese salted green pickles or 1 small can braised bamboo shoots
3 stalks spring onion
1 3½-oz can small button mushrooms
1 package frozen green peas
2–3 leaves crisp lettuce
2½ Tb vegetable oil
2 Tb butter
4 cups boiled rice
salt and pepper to taste

Preparation

After preparing the Soy Eggs, leave to cool in the sauce. When cold, dice in ¼-inch cubes. Chop the pickles and spring onions coarsely. Drain the liquid from the mushrooms. Thaw the peas. Cut lettuce leaves slantwise into 2–3 pieces.

Cooking and Serving

Heat the oil and butter in a large saucepan. When hot, add the mushrooms, pickles, and green peas. Stir fry together over medium heat for ½ minute. Add the lettuce and rice. Mix and stir fry for 1½ minutes. Sprinkle the ingredients in the pan with salt, pepper, and chopped eggs. Continue to stir fry, turn, and toss for 1½ minutes over medium heat. Serve in a well-heated bowl.

CHINESE SWEET RICE SALAD

2 – 3 oz beets
4-inch piece cucumber
4 – 5 oz cherries or seedless grapes
1 – 2 oranges or large mandarins
2 Tb soy sauce
3 tsp sugar
1½ Tb sherry
1½ Tb honey
2 Tb water
3½ Tb vegetable oil
1 Tb sesame oil
¼ lb raisins
4 cups cooked rice

Preparation
Trim the beets and dice into ¼-inch cubes. Dice the cucumber into the same size cubes, retaining the green skin. Remove the pits or seeds from the cherries or grapes. Peel the oranges and chop into small pieces. Mix the next 5 ingredients – the flavorers – in a bowl.

Cooking and Serving
Heat the vegetable oil and sesame oil in a large saucepan over medium heat. Add the beets, cucumber, and raisins. Turn in the oil for ¼ minute. Add the rice, and turn and toss in the oil with other ingredients for 1 minute. Add the cherries or grapes and oranges. Sprinkle the contents evenly with the flavoring ingredients from the bowl. Stir fry, turn, and toss for 1½ minutes more. Serve hot or cold.

SWEETS

CHINESE CUISINE is not particularly noted for its sweets, but there is a surprisingly large range of them. I am including a few recipes for sweets here, because such dishes are usually welcome after a succession of highly savory dishes. Chinese desserts are often served in the middle of a meal, sometimes in the form of a sweet soup, in order to break the sequence of savory dishes.

SWEET STEAMED DUMPLINGS

The process of making sweet steamed dumplings is the same as making savory Steamed Dumplings. The only difference lies in the stuffing. The favorite and most common Chinese sweet stuffings are sweet red-bean paste and sesame seeds stir fried with brown sugar. Sweet red-bean paste can be purchased in Chinese food shops. To use it as stuffing, you will need ½ pound paste or an equal amount of sesame seeds mixed with brown sugar. Stir fry in 1½ tablespoons vegetable oil and 1½ tablespoons butter for 4–5 minutes over low heat. Cool before using.

If sweet bean paste cannot be obtained, it can be made by gently boiling 1 pound red beans in 6 cups water for 2½ hours, stirring until all the husks float to the top. Skim off the husks and strain the liquid through cheesecloth. Squeeze the beans in the cloth until they are nearly dry. Heat them with 1 tablespoon sesame oil, 3 tablespoons butter, and 4–6 tablespoons brown sugar over gentle heat. Stir continually with a wooden spoon until the mixture is smooth and even, about 6–7 minutes.

Sweet sesame paste can be made by heating ⅔ pound sesame seeds with 5–6 tablespoons brown sugar, 3–4 tablespoons water, 1½ tablespoons sesame oil, 1½ tablespoons vegetable oil, and 2 tablespoons butter over very gentle heat for 8–9 minutes, stirring constantly until the mixture is smooth. This paste and the sweet bean paste are the two basic stuffings used in Chinese desserts. At festival times, these sweet steamed dumplings are tipped with red vegetable coloring and displayed on tables in mountainous heaps for the children to pick up and eat.

SWEET ORANGE TEA

Quite a few Chinese sweets occur in soup form. Although this may be strange to the Western palate, such "soups" make a refreshing change in a large Chinese meal with its succession of highly seasoned courses. This is one of them:

    4–5 oranges
    4 Tb sugar
    1 Tb cornstarch
    3 cups water

Preparation, Cooking, and Serving
Cut the oranges into halves and squeeze the juice from them. Put the water in a saucepan and add the sugar and cornstarch. Bring to a boil, stirring steadily. Add the orange juice and heat through. Serve in a large bowl placed in the center of the table or in small individual bowls. Good hot or chilled. For variation, stir in 1–2 tablespoons honey. Serves 4–6.

SWEET PINEAPPLE AND CHERRY TEA

Repeat the previous recipe, using a small can of pineapple
and ½ pound fresh pitted cherries. Heat them together with
cornstarch, sugar or honey, and water for 5 minutes. Serve in
a large bowl or divide the cherries, pineapple, and hot sug-
ared soup into small individual bowls.

SWEET ALMOND TEA

In contrast to the two previous "teas," which are like clear
soups, this is a thick one.

    3 cups water
    ½ lb almond meat or 6 Tb almond paste or ground almond
    4 Tb rice flour
    4 Tb sugar
    1 cup evaporated milk
    1 tsp almond extract

Preparation, Cooking, and Serving
Put the water in a heavy saucepan. Add the almond meat,
flour, and sugar. Bring to a boil, reduce the heat to a minimum, and put an asbestos pad under the pan. Continue to
heat, stirring occasionally, for ¼ hour. Add the evaporated
milk and almond extract. Stir and serve, as soon as it boils
again, in small individual bowls.

ALMOND JUNKET

    ¼ lb almond meat or 3 Tb ground almond
    1½ cups water
    2 packages gelatin
    4 Tb sugar
    1 6-oz can evaporated milk
    1 tsp almond extract

Preparation and Cooking
In a blender, grind the almond meat to a fine powder. Heat half the water and dissolve the gelatin in it.

Bring the rest of the water to the boil in a saucepan. Add the almond, dissolved gelatin, and sugar. Heat gently and stir for 5–6 minutes. Pour in the evaporated milk and almond extract. Heat until the mixture is about to boil again. Stir and remove from heat to cool. When somewhat cool, pour into a flat dish or pan, and place in the refrigerator to chill.

Serving
When the mixture has set firmly, cut into ½-inch cubes or diamond shapes, and serve with an equal amount of fresh and canned fruits. The nutty taste of almond gives an added dimension to a fruit salad. Alternatively, in China these almond cubes or diamonds are sometimes served on their own in sugary water or honeyed syrup.

HOT WALNUT SOUP

    1 lb walnut meat
    3 cups water
    4 – 5 Tb rice flour
    5 – 6 Tb sugar
    1 6-oz can evaporated milk

Preparation and Cooking
Grind the walnuts to a fine powder in a blender. Put the water in a saucepan. Add the powdered walnut and rice flour. Bring to a boil. Put an asbestos pad under the pan and simmer over very gentle heat for 15 minutes, stirring continuously. Add the sugar and evaporated milk. Stir until the mixture boils again.

Serving
Serve hot in 5 – 6 individual bowls.

FRIED LOTUS FLOWER

12 pieces lotus petal
4 – 5 Tb sweet bean paste
2 Tb plain flour
4 egg whites
2 – 3 Tb colored sugar
oil for deep frying

Preparation and Cooking
Clean and dry the petals and halve each one. Spread some bean paste on one of the half petals and cover with the other half to make a sandwich. Use up all the petals in this way.

Beat the egg whites and flour in a bowl until well blended. Dip the sandwiches in the egg and flour mixture, and place 4 at a time in a wire basket to deep fry for 2 minutes.

Serving
Arrange the lotus-petal sandwiches on a well-heated serving dish, sprinkle with colored sugar, and serve. Makes 12.

GLAZED CHESTNUTS

3 cups water
2 cups sugar
½ cup honey
1 lb chestnut meat or skinned chestnuts

Preparation and Cooking
Put the water in a heavy saucepan, and dissolve the sugar and honey in it over very low heat. When all the sugar has dissolved and the liquid becomes siruplike, add the chestnuts, putting an asbestos pad under the pan. Cook steadily for ¾ – 1 hour over very gentle heat, turning the chestnuts over now and then.

Serving

Place the chestnuts – separating them from one another – on a well-greased plate. Serve when cool.

Other kinds of nut, such as walnuts and lotus seeds, can be treated in the same way.

GLAZED POTATO CHIPS

The Peking brittle-glazed apple is becoming a fairly well-known sweet in Peking restaurants in the West, but potatoes can be treated in the same manner with surprising results.

    1 lb potatoes
    oil for deep frying
    6 heaping Tb sugar
    2 Tb honey
    2 Tb vegetable oil
    3 Tb water
    1 large glass bowl of iced water

Preparation and Cooking

Cut the potatoes into medium-size chips. Place them in a wire basket and deep fry them in 3 batches for 3 minutes each. Drain.

Gently heat the sugar, honey, vegetable oil, and water in a pan. Stir until the sugar has dissolved completely, stirring continually. Place an asbestos pad under the pan, and continue to heat gently for another 2 minutes. Add the potato chips, turning them in the sirup until every piece is well covered.

Serving

Separate the chips from one another. As soon as they are detached, drop them individually into the iced water. The sudden impact of coolness causes the film of sirup over each chip to form a brittle coating. They should be retrieved immediately from the water to prevent them from getting soggy, and eaten at once. The sensation of teeth cracking through the thin sweet covering is one of the pleasures of this dish.

For more conventional palates, exactly the same process can be followed with apples.

WATER-CHESTNUT JELLY

    3 – 4 pieces fresh or canned water chestnut
    8 Tb water-chestnut flour
    6 Tb sugar
    2 cups water
    2 envelopes gelatin
    cream

Preparation and Cooking
Slice the water chestnuts into thin matchsticks. Blend the water-chestnut flour with the sugar and water in a saucepan. Bring to a boil and simmer over low heat. Add the gelatin and stir for 1 minute.

Pour the mixture into a well-greased deep-sided flat-bottomed dish. Sprinkle the water-chestnut strips evenly over the mixture, and allow them to sink into the liquid. When cool, place the dish in the refrigerator for 2 – 3 hours, by which time the liquid should have set.

Serving
Turn the jelly onto a flat dish and cut into 6 even pieces. Serve each piece with some cream. The contrast between the texture of the shredded water chestnut and the water-chestnut jelly is stimulating to the palate. Serves 6.

CHILLED PEARS IN HONEY SIRUP

    6 firm pears
    1 1/2 cup sugar
    3 Tb honey
    1 – 2 Tb crème de menthe or other sweet liqueur

Preparation and Cooking
Peel the 6 pears, leaving the stem on for easy handling. Place them in a flat-bottomed pan and barely cover with water. Bring to the boil and simmer for 20 minutes. Pour off half the water and sprinkle the sugar over the pears. Simmer for another 20 minutes.

Arrange the pears on a deep-sided flat-bottomed dish. Spoon half the sirupy juice over the pears. Place the dish in the refrigerator to chill for 2 hours.

Serving
Add the honey and sweet liqueur to the remainder of the sirupy juice and stir until well blended. Cool in the refrigerator. When ready to serve pour the honey-liqueur sirup over each of the pears. Serves 6.

EIGHT PRECIOUS PUDDING

Finally, a kind of Chinese Christmas pudding made with rice!

  ½ cup lotus nuts
  ½ cup walnuts
  ¼ cup melon-seed meat (optional)
  2 cups water
  6 Tb sugar
  4 Tb butter or margarine
  2 cups glutinous rice
  ¼ cup honey dates
  ¼ cup cherry glacé
  ¼ cup green candied fruits
  ¼ cup dried dragon's eyes (*loon ngaan*)
  ¼ cup orange or red candied peel
  1 cup bean paste

Preparation
Blanch the nuts. Add 2 cups water, sugar and 1 tablespoon butter to the rice. Bring to a boil and heat very gently, with an asbestos pad under the pan, until the rice is almost com-

pletely dry. Chop the dates and candied fruits into halves or quarters.

Heavily grease the sides of a large mold or bowl with the remainder of the butter, and cover with a ¼-inch layer of rice. Stud the rice with the peel, dates, candied fruits, and nuts, pushing them through the walls of the rice. Fill the mold with alternate layers of rice and bean paste, making each succeeding layer of rice 3 or 4 times the thickness of the paste, and studding each layer of rice with the remainder of the candied fruits, nuts, peel, and dates. The final layer should be rice.

Cooking
Place the mold or bowl in a steamer, and steam steadily for 60–70 minutes.

Serving
Turn the pudding onto a dish, and serve as you would serve a Christmas pudding.

Index

About the Author

KENNETH H. C. LO has been a news commentator for the BBC, a diplomat, a fine-arts publisher, a champion tennis player, and most recently a cookery writer and food critic. He is the author of *Peking Cooking* (Pantheon, 1973).